The Best Rock-and-Roll Records of All Time

THE BEST ROCK-and-ROLL RECORDS OF ALL TIME

A Fan's Guide to the Stuff You Love

by Jimmy Guterman

A Citadel Press Book
Published by Carol Publishing Group

Copyright © 1992 by Jimmy Guterman

A Citadel Press Book
Published by Carol Publishing Group
Citadel Press is a registered trademark of Carol Communications, Inc.

Editorial Offices   Sales & Distribution Offices
600 Madison Avenue   120 Enterprise Avenue
New York, NY 10022   Secaucus, NJ 07094

In Canada: Canadian Manda Group
P.O. Box 920, Station U,
Toronto, Ontario M8Z 5P9

Queries regarding rights and permissions
should be addressed to: Carol Publishing Group,
600 Madison Avenue, New York, NY 10022

Manufactured in the United States of America

10 9 8 7 6 5 4 3 2 1

Carol Publishing Group books are available at special discounts
for bulk purchases, for sales promotions, fund raising, or
educational purposes. Special editions can also be created to
specifications. For details contact: Special Sales Department,
Carol Publishing Group, 120 Enterprise Ave., Secaucus, NJ 07094

Library of Congress Cataloging-in-Publication Data

Guterman, Jimmy.
    The best rock-and-roll records of all time / by Jimmy Guterman.
      p.   cm.
    "A Citadel Press book."
    ISBN 0-8065-1325-X (paper)
    1. Rock music—Miscellanea.   2. Rock music—Discography.
  I. Title.
  ML3534.G87   1992
  782.42166′026′6—dc20
                                                          92-7896
                                                              CIP
                                                              MN

For Jane Kokernak

Contents

Acknowledgments
Author's Note
The Best

CONTENTS

CONTENTS

Acknowledgments

For continuing encouragement and support, I am grateful to Mark Caro, Charlie Conrad, Kath Hansen, Andrew McLenon, Tim Riley, Steve Sloan, and Dave Yeskel. All these people also submit to engaging me in frequent arguments about pop music, for which they all deserve long vacations in places that have no telephones.

At Carol, thanks for last time and once again to Steven Schragis, Bruce Bender, Steven Brower, Ben Petrone and everyone in publicity, and my editor Gail Kinn.

Owen O'Donnell was officially my partner on *The Worst Rock and Roll Records of All Time* and he is my accomplice (i.e., unindictable co-conspirator) on almost everything else. The book you are holding is only my side of the conversation, so you can't blame him this time. Thanks also to the DeFazio-Kramer family, Amy Goldstein, and Ed McCarthy.

More personal thanks to John Guterman, Deanna and Ed Schey, a lot of people with the last name Kokernak, Brent E. Sparks, Martha Mulligan, Eric Hooper, Annie Hooper, Jane Popofsky, Sybil Carey, Richard Piazza, and Amelia Piazza.

Author's Note

When I sat down with my friend Owen O'Donnell to write *The Worst Rock and Roll Records of All Time,* we proceeded from the thesis that rock criticism (not even rock *and roll* criticism, a change in terminology which should tell you something about pretentiousness) had gotten too stuffy for its own good—or for the good of the music we love so much. The reaction to that book ranged from polite bemusement to outright hate, so I figured I'd go at it again. Go figure.

I'm still troubled by the polite, enthusiasm-free Zeitgeist so common in writing about pop music, particularly in the major publications that claim to cover the field. Even if a critic says he or she likes a record, it's hard to know if the record prompted any enjoyment, or any reaction at all. Just as I did with Owen a few years ago, this time I wanted to write about records that made me respond, inspired me in some way. Just as anyone can make a bad album without trying, most credible rock and rollers can record a pretty good one without great exertion. I wanted to probe the extremes, force myself to choose which albums made me react most intently (in a positive way), and figure out why. Just for fun, I ranked them too, from my absolute favorite on down to my hundredth favorite.

It's more difficult writing about records you love than records you detest. Humor isn't as effective a critical weapon and it's even more important to focus on the work and not its accoutrements. But it's more fun: listening to *Exile on Main Street* over and over is undoubtedly a more pleasurable experience than repeated exposure to Jethro Tull albums. I'm writing here most of all about records that give me great pleasure, and to keep myself honest I limit myself to one record from each artist. Otherwise this would be a book about my favorite Rolling Stones and Otis Redding records, and although this book is hopelessly incomplete as a history of rock and roll, that would have been taking matters too far. In art, pleasure need not be an activity that produces a smile: Films as great as *The Night of the Hunter* or books as great as *London Fields* elate us even if darkness is the source of their drawing power. Albums as desperate as *Astral Weeks* and *Nebraska* are worthy going back to time and again as much as lighthearted masterpieces like the Contours' *Do You Love Me* or Rockpile's *Seconds of Pleasure.*

As I gradually narrowed my choices, I noticed some disturbing statistical aberrations. The nature of long-playing albums, which is that they are intended for a more well-off audience than that of singles, makes a listing of great records both whiter and maler than a singles listing or a roundup of favorite artists. Barely half the records here (I use the terms "album" and "record" interchangeably) are by African-American performers, which is absurd considering the extent of African-American contributions to rock and roll, and a pitiful less than one-fourth of these records are by women. There is great music made by people of every persuasion (except art-rockers, of course), though choosing albums rather than singles as a measure results in a more conservative pool.

This book could easily have been five hundred records or five thousand records, but I don't want to overstay my welcome. In this volume, I use a broad definition of rock and roll, including work by many overt blues, country, and reggae performers, though I can only stretch the idea so far. For instance, I love the Willie Nelson and Webb Pierce duet album *In the Jailhouse Now*, but that record does not belong here nor does Howlin' Wolf's *Change My Way* or J. B. Lenoir's *Natural Man*. Also, this is a book about favorite records, not favorite performers. Folks as varied as Fats Domino and Tom Petty have made many fine LPs, but not one beginning-to-end great one. Similarly, some great singles artists—the Sex Pistols, Claudine Clark, Lou Christie, to name a few— hardly even tried long-players. I also tried to stay away from box sets, unless the stories those overpriced boxes told were grander and more worth hearing than that on any original-issue album.

These records talk to each other, and listening to several of these records in concert with others should be more revealing. Strange juxtapositions occur on this list, just as they do in record collections, or life: Bob Marley standing next to Hank Williams Jr. is funny, if nothing else. It was also fascinating to discover that many disparate performers cut versions of the same song. Such "cover" versions help define the common language that these one hundred albums share.

Finally, several people have asked me what Number One Hundred and One would have been. Randy Newman's *12 Songs* was the last record I took off the list, although there are many Booker T. and the MG's and Bobby Bland records that should be here. *Back To Mono* would have made it, but it came out too late for inclusion. And what about *Music From Big Pink*? Here I strip my tastes to the essence and find out what means the most to me. I hope these records are enriching to you too. At the very least, thanks for indulging me.

The Best Rock-and-Roll Records of All Time

Number One

Rod Stewart
Every Picture Tells a Story
Mercury, 1971

One of the cardinal myths of rock and roll is that it's nothing more than black music played by white people. Such an assertion is usually an attempt to cast aspersions on either the source (as played by a black, the stuff was too rough to deserve a hearing) or the recipient (the whites just stole it). The truth is that white boys learned about the blues and loved it so much that they sought to make sense of it in their own language. This may be counterintuitive but it is also indisputable. Elvis Presley and Jerry Lee Lewis in Memphis, Buddy Holly in Clovis: These hillbilly cats knew that they didn't belong in existing structures, that they had to create a new world built on the music they heard on the wrong sides of the tracks in their respective hometowns.

This all got started in July 1954, when Elvis Presley, Scotty Moore, and Bill Black tore through an Arthur Crudup blues tune, "That's All Right," under the supervision of Sun Records owner Sam Phillips. "That's different," Phillips said while they played it back. "That's a pop song now." Not quite: It resembled nothing on the pop radio stations of the day. What Phillips meant by "pop song" was that this new version wasn't quite country, wasn't quite blues. It was . . . different, but it was something that Phillips immediately sensed would move both blues and country folk. That's why it was a "pop song."

One of the most vivid tracks on Rod Stewart's *Every Picture Tells a Story* is a hard-edged "That's All Right," based on the Elvis, Scotty, and Bill version. It rocks harder, thanks to the Cro-Magnon drumming of Mick Waller, the leviathan guitars of Stewart, Ron Wood, and Martin Quittenton, and Stewart's distinctive rasp cajoling, charming, testifying, and dancing. The elemental backup, tight and unstudied, gladly cedes room

1

to Stewart, unlike most of the electric British hard rock of the time. Singer and band travel up and down together, through inside jokes (such as a quote from an older Stewart composition) and perilous key changes. This is a song he's known for fifteen years and Elvis's version is on a record that Rod has sung along with for all that time. Conscious of it or not, Stewart understands the breakthrough that Elvis pulled off in the Memphis Recording Service. He knows the extent and ramifications of what Elvis invented. He wants to be Elvis, an icon so overwhelming that even a British kid like Rod can identify with it.

Every Picture Tells a Story is Stewart's bid for rock-and-roll immortality, an ambitious record in a variety of senses (he wants Elvis's wallet as well as his gifts) and dwarfs other such attempts, even successful ones like Jimi Hendrix's *Are You Experienced?* and Bruce Springsteen's *Born in the U.S.A.* Stewart's third solo album is an all-encompassing work: Stewart demands attention from everyone on every level. His imaginative songwriting is rife with telling detail: The hair-combing scene in "Every Picture Tells a Story," the morning-after madness in "Maggie May," and the weather report in "Mandolin Wind" are all the products of a man in love with the world and his ability to describe that world and reassure himself.

The performances exceed the writing, especially on the outside tunes, which thrive on Stewart's devotion to them. "(I Know) I'm Losing You" is a hard-rock version of the Temptations hit that Stewart recorded with his sometime band the Faces. Stewart knows not to mimic the Motown original: He accepts the Sun dictum that personal expression far outlasts attempts to copy, that copying is in itself not merely fruitless but intolerable. Stewart puts across Tim Hardin's "(Find a) Reason to Believe" as an organ-driven call for moxie in the face of resignation, and on the mostly acoustic take on Bob Dylan's aching "Tomorrow Is a Long Time," Stewart is even more determined. Most of the time, the characters in *Every Picture Tells a Story* find themselves in a desperate condition, and what upraises them is the confidence of the narrator.

Such endurance is most apparent on "Every Picture Tells a Story" and "Maggie May," a pair of shattering acoustic hard-rock numbers about young men (or old boys, your call) gaining experience in ways they never expected or intended. These two songs, among the most durable pop-music offerings of the century, are so bold, so honest about their doubts, so willing and able to transcend their immediate difficulties, that they fulfill the dreams Woody Guthrie gave life to in "Bound for Glory." On

2

Every Picture Tells a Story, Rod Stewart is as undeniable, as welcome, as any singer will ever be. It's no wonder that this record made Stewart's dreams come true (not to mention the aspirations of his fans). Stewart is phenomenally rich now, but his records stink (also, he has recently ruined "Every Picture Tells a Story" for many by selling it to a beer company). As *Every Picture Tells a Story* reminds you at every turn, he once had it all. And that's no fairy tale.

Number Two

The Rolling Stones
Exile on Main Street
Rolling Stones, 1972

Mud: That's the word that best describes *Exile on Main Street*, a double-album chronicling the scarifying morning after the heady sixties finally slammed shut. The Rolling Stones are the greatest band in the history of rock and roll, greater than the Beatles mostly because they lasted longer (it's no accident that the Stones' peak years came after the Beatles were safely out of the way). But there is mud all over everything here: words are mumbled, indistinguishable sound washes between speakers like waves of fog, and when clear ideas do inadvertently pop up, they seem worn and blurred. More than anything else, this is a record about imagination in the face of the sixties' collapse.

The Rolling Stones had already traveled farther than any band when they recorded this masterpiece of grunge. Except for *Their Satanic Majesties Request*, their brief, unfortunate flirtation with psychedelia (while the Beatles were around, their influence extended even to the Stones), all the albums the Rolling Stones recorded, from *Around and Around* to *Sticky Fingers*, were full of trashy vitality, enlivened versions of soul and blues classics side by side with the most brilliant, nasty distillations of lust and rebellion the band could imagine. But the Rolling Stones were a significantly different band in 1971, when they recorded *Exile on Main Street*, than they were in their salad days. For one thing, they had fired the man who started the band, Brian Jones, who promptly drugged himself into oblivion and death. For another, their age was dragging on them. Nowadays rockers in their late twenties seem relatively young, but in 1971 a twenty-eight-year-old rocker seemed ancient. The Rolling Stones felt old when they recorded this record, and they found solace in the blues.

4

Mick Jagger sings lead on all but one number here, and his performances are his steadiest and least affected ever. Much of this double-record was recorded in the basement of guitarist Keith Richards's house, and the informal surroundings saw to it that Mick didn't prance (the unlikely setting also contributed to the muddy sound). Mick talks directly. And Keith! Keith Richards is the greatest harmony singer in the history of rock and roll, mostly because he is the only one who can sing in several keys at the same time. Like his Fender lines, his voice darts through spaces in arrangements and fills without cluttering. His solo vocal piece, "Happy," is one of the lighter songs on *Exile on Main Street,* though the chorus line "I need love to keep me happy" is a pretty damn desperate one under the right circumstances.

Of course, that's assuming you can get at the words. After you figure out all the lyrics—a task that takes years—then you have to figure out what they mean, which is impossible. "I only get my rocks off while I'm sleeping," "My mouth don't move but I can hear you speak," "The sunshine bores the daylights out of me": Those lines are all from only the first of these eighteen dissolute compositions. Sex and independence are the major issues here, but what comes through clearer than any words (except on "All Down the Line" and a luxurious cover version of Robert Johnson's "Stop Breaking Down") are the caressing bass of Bill Wyman and the shotgun drums of Charlie Watts. The music completely overpowers the lyrics on *Exile on Main Street.* You decipher "Wham bam, throw a ham/Alabam don't give a damn"; I'll just sing along.

When its advocates term *Exile on Main Street* one of the sleaziest albums of all time, we're not only talking about the words. Producer Jimmy Miller has since disowned the sound of this record, blaming its sonic impenetrability on recording circumstances. But how this record sounds is inextricable from what it's whispering behind its mammoth snarl. Be it an all-out rocker like "All Down the Line," a frank blues like "Let It Loose," or a dark fusion of the two like "Torn and Frayed," the Rolling Stones turn *Exile on Main Street* into an extended deliberation on how to live like teenagers forever. For all its maturity, *Exile on Main Street* is about grown men discovering that the road can go on forever, though they now know that the price will be horribly high. So when the occasional line does leap out—"You can be my partner in crime" is about the friendliest—such an existence seems not only desirable but necessary, even if it is drenched in doubt, fear, and mud.

Number Three

Van Morrison
Astral Weeks
Warner Brothers, 1968

The mystery of love, the love of mystery: Throughout Van Morrison's career, the two notions circle each other and coalesce, swirling, until Morrison steps back, restarting the process. The title of one of Morrison's most enduring songs, "Into the Mystic," articulates this journey ("Into the Mystic" is on *Moondance*, a brilliant album except for its phenomenally overrated supper-club title track). *Astral Weeks* is Morrison's first solo album after leaving Them and cutting some random sessions for Bang that yielded a Top Ten hit in "Brown Eyed Girl." It's drastically different from anything Van the Man had tried in the past or would attempt in the future. (In terms of sustained intensity, only *St. Dominic's Preview, Veedon Fleece,* and *Into the Music* come close to *Astral Weeks*, though all of Morrison's albums offer some tracks worth hearing.)

On *Astral Weeks*, Morrison and his band, a hastily assembled jazz combo featuring the masterful melodic bassist Richard Davis, hunt for a place beyond words, a peaceful home safe from the tyranny of language. Yet *Astral Weeks* glides away from jazz into its own world. I must acknowledge that my knowledge of post-1930 jazz only slightly exceeds my fluency in Sanskrit, but anyone with ears knows that most fusions of jazz and rock incorporate the worst elements of both musical forms; the results are usually formless, overorchestrated, and too loud. *Astral Weeks* is perhaps the only overt jazz-rock mix that works, in part because its sparse settings are ideal counterpoints to the lyrics. Whatever the connection to jazz, *Astral Weeks* still aspires to pop. Pop music is inherently repetitive, and Morrison extends this idea to his words, and then to extremes. The lyrical repetitions on *Astral Weeks* surpass even those of James Brown, as Van expresses his roundabout visions with quiet inten-

6

sity: "You breathe in you breathe out you breathe in you breathe out you breathe in you breathe out you breathe in you breathe out" and "You turn around you turn around you turn around you turn around" from "Beside You," a diffuse tune about some of the redemptive powers of sex, are but two of the many examples. Morrison stretches the tunes, flexes the ideas, until they give him something he senses as new.

When Van does get around to relating stories, he can't. The details are too sketchy. His narrators are too close to their material to step back and comment on their actions; they are imprisoned by their desires. "Cyprus Avenue" is *Lolita* as narrated by an unreflecting Humbert Humbert watching the girls walk by from his car seat, too paralyzed to move; "Madame George," which takes place on the same street, observes a party (down to the "click and clack of the high-heeled shoes") and identifies intensely with a ridiculed transvestite before Van cries, "That's when you fall/that's when you fall/when you fall into a trance" and the action returns to Van's most favored landscape: His own mind, where he resolves to move on as strings carry him away. This is an insular record, though apparently not by choice. No wonder the wily John Lee Hooker cuts duets with him. Neither of them can get out of the blues alive.

Number Four

James Brown
Star Time
Polydor, 1991

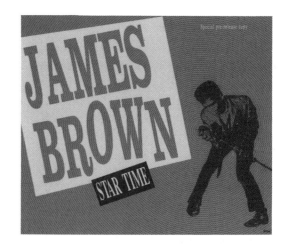

Wow!

Although our shelves are weighed down more and more with boxed sets, this one is a must. In recent years, no major artist of the fifties and sixties has been better served by a major label than James Brown. Great compilations by Soul Brother Number One appear with startling frequency and probably will for years to come. Until this five-hour extravaganza showed up, the pick was probably *Roots of a Revolution.*

Even before he started to transform pop in 1965 with his first two Top Ten hits, "Papa's Got a Brand New Bag" and "I Got You (I Feel Good)," the Godfather of Soul had a decade's worth of thorny, seminal proto-soul behind him as well as a gigantic following in the African-American community. *Roots of a Revolution,* compiled by U.K. James Brown expert Cliff White, concentrates on the years 1956 to 1964, and indeed documents what its title proclaims. Across these tracks, you can hear rhythmic and melodic gifts develop and overlap; you can hear confidence accrue and explode. Early songs reveal some unexpected influences ("Connie-on-Chon" suggests Little Richard fronting Louis Jordan's Tympani Five); by the end of the set, recordings like "Prisoner of Love" and "(Do the) Mashed Potatoes" scream a talent that won't be denied, can't be contained.

It can hardly be contained in the four-CD *Star Time,* either. Although petulant fans might consider the set incomplete (why not ten CDs, they ask), this is the crowning achievement (so far, anyway) in PolyGram's James Brown reissue program. Chronological order is usually a straitjacket in box sets, forcing compilers to favor a calendar over ideas. But Brown is a restless soul (or soul man) who as recently as the mid-eighties was searching for new ways to express his visions, so the chronological setup lets us hear him develop, expand, collapse, turnabout, retrench, and explode, over and over again. The set starts in the *Roots of a Revolution* period and ends with "Unity," a duet with hip-hop pioneer Afrika Bambaataa that underlines how many generations Brown has inspired. And he upstages Bambaataa with ease.

Star Time is full of emotions better expressed in a scream or a cry than words. Indeed, verbal facility takes a backseat to direct emotional expression, although some of the song titles here suggest a fertile lyrical mind: "I Don't Want Nobody to Give Me Nothing (Open Up the Door I'll Get It Myself)," "Get Up, Get Into It, and Get Involved," and so on. As with Van Morrison's language never gets in the way of Brown's ideas; the preconscious notions about relationships, politics, and rhythms that run through *Star Time* work themselves out in the music—extended, single-chord marches in which lyrical elaboration would be superfluous. Throughout *Star Time* James Brown argues that one taut rhythm, even one confined to permutations of one firm chord, can say more about motion and emotion than the most complex run of chord changes. His vision of music is stripped to the marrow, as direct as a punch or a kiss. And through the five hours of *Star Time* there isn't a moment that undermines the method.

Number Five

Otis Redding
Dictionary of Soul
Volt, 1966

Five albums on, only twenty-five years old, Otis Redding had already transcended ideas of what soul music could include. Aside from his startling, borderline-hoarse shouting, he had developed into a superlative songwriter, producer, pianist, and talent scout. His own compositions stretched the bounds of the form, and his choices of outside numbers to perform—particularly the Rolling Stones' rocker "(I Can't Get No) Satisfaction"—suggested that anyone committed enough to soul who had enough verve and imagination could add virtually anything to the tradition. (No doubt Al Green must have been listening somewhere.)

Every Otis Redding album released in his lifetime (and a good number of the posthumous ones) breathed love and fire, although the uncharacteristically light *King and Queen,* a duet record with Carla Thomas (surpassed in the form only by Marvin Gaye and Tammi Terrell), and *Otis Blue,* which featured his original version of "Respect" and a devastating reading of William Bell's "You Don't Miss Your Water," seem most lively as albums, not merely singles collections. But *Dictionary of Soul* featured not only a wider array of bared influences (Chuck Willis, the country standard "Tennessee Waltz," and the Beatles' "Day Tripper") as well as the usual groundbreaking Redding originals, but also some of the best-ever playing by the greatest house band in the history of rock and roll. Perhaps this record really should be called *Booker T. and the MGs' Greatest Hits.*

Based around the MGs (Booker T. on organ, Steve Cropper on guitar, Donald "Duck" Dunn on bass, Al Jackson on drums) and the Memphis Horns (Wayne Jackson on trumpet, Andrew Love and Floyd Newman on saxophones), this band, usually sympathetic and careful to service the song at all costs, worked especially close with the singer on arrangements, and it shows. The horns were especially well integrated into the MG's crisp, clipped rhythms on a number of songs including the midtempo "Fa-Fa-Fa-Fa-Fa (Sad Song)," the salvation-offering ballad "Try a Little Tenderness," and the uptempo soul-rockers that round out the album ("She Put the Hurt on Me," the arch "Love Have Mercy").

Redding, of course, more than carried his own weight, howling like a Delta bluesman in the down-and-dirty "Hawg for You," laughing and rhyming "toe" and "more" before a strutting horn-and-guitar break in "Sweet Lorene," singing with less restraint and less worry than ever before all over the record. Listening to *Dictionary of Soul*, it's easy to imagine the band as they look at Redding, following him through unexpected changes, committed to him like a mother to a child. You can almost sense them leaning toward him. Otis Redding deserved such treatment; if you want to personify soul, here's your man.

Number Six

Jerry Lee Lewis
Live at the Star-Club
Philips, 1964

Jerry Lee Lewis, the Killer, was on an upswing in early 1964. "I'm on Fire," featured his most lively, elemental rock and roll since he left Sun Records the previous year. He returned to London, the site of his great scandal, and triumphed. On April 5, 1964, he played at the Star-Club on Reeperbahn, Hamburg, a performance preserved on an LP released only in Germany. Before he began shouting the first song, Jerry Lee rolled his tongue at the audience, warming up his voice and his attitude; he did not wait for the opening note to start performing. Though Jerry Lee's recordings on Sun (collected on the *Classic* boxed set) and under Huey Meaux's ostensible supervision (the amazing 1974 LP *Southern Roots*) were his greatest, his real peak was before a live audience. An American live album recorded around the same time as *Live at the Star-Club* was called *The Greatest Live Show on Earth*, and it was. Yet somehow *Live at the Star-Club* was even more ferocious.

The kick-off tune, "Mean Woman Blues," was leery, malicious, frenetic, everything Jerry Lee's blues-soaked version of rock and roll offered or implied. An exhilarating "High School Confidential" climaxed in a tense piano solo, and "Money" went far beyond the recorded version. Sultry, primitive, demanding, Jerry Lee ignored his band and wrenched all he could from the ugly truths at the song's center. The breakdown before the final charge featured some defiant scatting in which Jerry Lee said everything that needed to be conveyed in wordless taunts that no one could have misunderstood. "Matchbox" was his first attempt at a Carl Perkins performance that exceeded the model. Jerry Lee defined the tune as an agreeable strut and was so taken by himself that he kept soloing through the guitar interlude and derived extra pleasure from singing, "If you don't like my peaches/Please don't shake my tree."

The Ray Charles number "What'd I Say" at the Star-Club was one of the three or four most amazing performances of Jerry Lee's career. From its far-ranging piano introduction through some screaming that took in a lifetime's worth of disappointment and frustration, it jumped into an extended coda that was at once both generous and utterly sleazy. "Down the Line" maintained the scorching pace with a strong, rough delivery of lines like, "I'm gonna do right/And you'd better believe that Jerry Lee is gonna do right."

"Jerry! Jerry!" the crowd chanted; the object of their affection took up the chant; and everyone vaulted into a "Great Balls of Fire" that should have set off the smoke detectors, with Jerry Lee's eternal argument setting off explosions at every turn. "Good Golly Miss Molly" was wilder even than Little Richard's, and "Lewis Boogie" was an ideal, implosive pumping-piano showcase, marvelous tension implied by the band's heated attempt to keep up with the Killer. It went on and on, flexible, soulful, undeniable. Somewhere tonight, Jerry Lee is onstage and to some degree that show continues.

Number Seven

Aretha Franklin
*I Never Loved a Man the Way
I Love You*
Atlantic, 1967

Aretha Franklin enjoys an iconic presence in pop music. Whenever a new vocalist comes up from the ranks who has a strong, malleable voice and an assertive presence, someone (usually a critic who has been fed the line by a publicist) labels the newcomer "the Aretha of rap," "the Aretha of country," or some such hype. Especially when a new soul singer arrives, she is inevitably compared to the Queen of Soul. (Sorry, Whitney.)

Franklin is a towering talent. Most of her records since the mid-seventies have been duds (though, in prime Jackie Wilson form, she still sings great in the midst of a travestied arrangement), but all her early Atlantic studio albums—*Aretha Arrives, Lady Soul, Aretha Now, Spirit in the Dark,* and *Amazing Grace*—remain among the purest, most colossal distillations ever of gospel-soul. Anyone producing Franklin should have recognized that a connection to gospel music was necessary if Aretha was to relax and be inspired in the studio. Aretha grew up in the church, but this was lost on her producers at Columbia, including the usually astute John Hammond. Jerry Wexler knew better; the Atlantic vice president, whose production and artists-and-repertoire skills were crucial to the label's soul-music hegemony, knew that Franklin's Columbia records weren't up to her singing and piano skills, so he picked up her contract, brought her down to Muscle Shoals, Alabama, and let her run free toward the music she loved virtually from birth.

Franklin delivered immediately. Her debut album for Atlantic, *I Never Loved a Man the Way I Love You,* is as meteoric a vocal set as any. Freed from others' ideas of what she should do—no one at Atlantic talked of the jazz market, the supper-club market, or any other useless demographic

14

information—Aretha got to sing songs she wrote, as well as material like Dan Penn and Chips Moman's "Do Right Woman–Do Right Man" and Sam Cooke's "Good Times" and "A Change Is Gonna Come" that she could invigorate.

Aretha's individual method is best exemplified by "Respect," her cover of the Otis Redding hit that starts *I Never Loved a Man the Way I Love You.* Horns and guitars swirl around her, loud and strong, but Franklin's voice and piano part the accompaniment like the Red Sea. Everything else is pushed back when Aretha arrives, no matter how sympathetic the backing. She takes total control, with an audacity that's one part gospel and ten parts rock and roll.

Strangely for someone heralded for her power, many of Franklin's strongest performances, both on this album and throughout her career, are outright expressions of dependence, "You're a no-good heartbreaker/You're a liar and a cheat" is the first couplet of "I Never Loved a Man (The Way I Love You)," "Dr. Feelgood (Love Is a Serious Business)" all but equates a lover with an illicit drug, and behind the "Gloria" chord changes in "Save Me" is a desperate singer. But these performances are exemplars of strength, of someone owning up to her own foibles and trying to get past them. For all its tender moments, *I Never Loved a Man the Way I Love You* is an album about struggle. On her first real album, Aretha Franklin presents herself as a woman who may be oppressed but will never accept the status quo.

Number Eight

Chuck Berry
The Chess Box
MCA, 1988

Chuck Berry is the greatest lyricist in the history of rock and roll. His unprecedented synthesis—blues (especially the jump-band variety), country, and swing funneled through his wry, nonlinear mind—extended ideas about what the new teen form could encompass. Berry took over rock and roll moments after its birth, and anyone who has subsequently picked up a guitar with the desire to write a rock-and-roll song that described real life knows that Berry provided most of the tools. He also coined the word "motorvatin'," which counts for a lot 'round these parts.

The Chess Box is a three-CD set that has a bit of fluff toward the end (Owen O'Donnell and I have already weighed in on "My Ding-a-Ling," although I'm pleased to report that the shorter single version is the darkening entity here), but that leaves more than sixty-five cuts showcasing Berry in his prime, all train-track guitar lines and images of "coffee-colored Cadillacs." Berry's prime musical foil is his St. Louis compatriot Johnnie Johnson, a pianist with a blues background whose rhythmic style was so flexible and skeptical that it influenced Chuck's fret work, not to mention his lyrical world-view. Piano and guitar hop over each other throughout this set, like grinning duelists. Detractors often claim that Berry's songs "all sound the same," but they're referring only to the jump-start guitar introductions that were Berry's duck-walking trademark—though even those were immediately distinguishable to seasoned fans. There's a tremendous variety of styles on *The Chess Box:* Listen to "Havana Moon," "School Day," "Dear Dad," and "Have Mercy Judge" and hear a performer able to thrive in blues, rhythm and blues, straight rock and roll, and his own fusion of them all. The only thing that's the same is the high quality.

16

Like Jerry Lee Lewis, Berry alternated between adult and teen topics as surely as he moved from adult to teen beats. Sometimes he could call up lines like the hilarious hyperboles in "No Money Down" (by the end of the song, he has an entire furniture store installed inside his brand-new car) that rang true and immediate to both. Berry's conversational singing is a major part of his appeal—everyone can understand what he is singing, although some couplets like "it's way too early for the Congo/So keep a'rockin' the piano" (from "Rock-and-Roll Music") have defied attempts at explication for decades.

On these recordings for *Chess*, Berry presented himself as a guy next door with a penchant for pungent and detailed singing, writing, and guitar-playing. He always considered himself an artist (he allowed none of the usual "It's junk because it's for kids" crap), and the most amazing thing about the wildly imaginative work throughout *The Chess Box* is that there's no condescension. Although the kids in the audience couldn't comprehend the singer's child-custody anguish in "Memphis," Berry wrote the tune in such an open-ended way that everyone could be included.

Number Nine

Prince
Sign o' the Times
Paisley Park/Warner Brothers, 1987

Ambition has never been a problem for Prince. From the start, the teenaged one-man-band sought to set convention on its head and create an alternate universe in which he, a self-perceived misfit, could make a home. *Dirty Mind* (1980) was the record that made everyone take notice. Although it remains Prince's only album not to spawn any hit pop singles, *Dirty Mind* was an unprecedented set that established Prince as a visionary, both musically in his extension of existing funk production methods and lyrically in his depiction of a world in which sex existed in a vacuum. In Prince's alternate universe, sex was all pleasure, with no responsibilities and no complications. On record (and, one senses, in real life as well) Prince still lives in this world where heady musical experimentation and frank, funny expressions of lust are what matter the most.

Although he established his unalterable agenda on *Dirty Mind*, that doesn't mean Prince hasn't progressed since then, taking in all sorts of musical sources—from Miles Davis to Public Enemy—and carnal themes (his recent video work suggests an overfamiliarity with the film *Caligula*). The double-album *Sign o' the Times* now stands as Prince's high-water mark on disc, although he records so frequently and so consistently that this could change at any moment.

For now, what elevates *Sign o' the Times* is its breadth, both lyrically (although Prince's id runs rampant here, there are also examinations of life as lived with one's clothes on) and musically (sources here are as disparate as Joni Mitchell, the Velvet Underground, and Parliament). It's Prince's finest record because it's the only one that acknowledges the outside world before transcending it. The record's roaming title track is best known for the dour list of travails in its barbed lyrics, though its sharp

18

drum-machine-and-guitar coda are what really set the tone for the sixteen-track set.

Although all of Prince's post-*Dirty Mind* albums have yielded massive pop hits, all of these records are also defiantly experimental. Megastardom has certainly changed Prince's life and encouraged his natural predilection to hermeticism, but it hasn't satisfied him creatively—perhaps nothing will. *Sign o' the Times* is full of his trademark idiosyncratic, galvanic funk ("Housequake," "It," "Hot Thing," the epic "It's Gonna Be a Beautiful Night," among others), as well as a hard-rock Jesus song ("The Cross," which sounds like the Staple Singers fronting the Velvets), a blazing duet that for the only time in her career makes sense of Sheena Easton ("U Got the Look"), and half a dozen numbers that revel in their uncategorizability.

Cut after he jettisoned his band the Revolution, *Sign o' the Times* has a "produced, arranged, composed, and performed by Prince" credit, but as its title suggests it's the one Prince album that acknowledges not only the existence of the outside world, but the possibility that someone in that outside world might have a different way of looking at things than Prince and that such alternate versions of the world might be acceptable. This last element is most evident in "If I Was Your Girlfriend," a downtempo kitchen-sink production number—it leads off with a church-organ flourish—in which Prince struggles with ideas about sexuality different from his own. *Sign o' the Times* has it both ways: It takes on the whole world, yet every song in one way or another connects to Prince's favorite subjects (sex, bubble baths, dancing, sex). Prince knows it—he sings "I think about it all the time"—but then discovers how far his beats and his mind can take him.

Sign o' the Times heralded the beginning of a particularly fertile period in Prince's career. Its follow-up, *The Black Album*, was pulled from release by Prince shortly before release in favor of the more overtly spiritual *Lovesexy*, although it is easily available in the usual surreptitious channels. It doesn't have anywhere near the breadth of *Sign o' the Times* but it is Prince's most charming straight funk album since *Dirty Mind*. As Prince says on the record, in a tip of the hat to Parliament's "Supergroovalisticprosifunkstication," *The Black Album* is nothing so much as "Superfunkycalifragisexi." Track it down, or write a nasty letter to Warner Brothers.

19

Number Ten

The Clash
London Calling
Epic, 1979

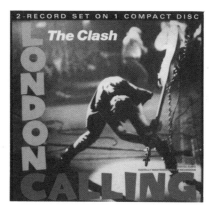

The Clash were already the best rock-and-roll band in the world—the Rolling Stones had long since peaked—when they recorded *London Calling*. Their homonymous debut album (worth owning in both its overlapping U.S. and U.K. configurations) made the Sex Pistols sound gutless in comparison (the Clash's anger had an end beyond its means), and in songs like "White Man in Hammersmith Palais" and Junior Murvin's "Police and Thieves," they expanded even the most optimistic notions of what punk could include without selling out. "We're a garage band/We come from Garageland," sneered singer Joe Strummer, but from the start they were much more. Mick Jones was that rare guitarist who didn't turn dull as his technical expertise blossomed (that is, he didn't succumb to Eric Clapton Disease), and the open songs he and Strummer hammered out made the nihilism of their fellow punks sound silly. From the beginning, they were pushing limits.

What remains most amazing about *London Calling*, a sixty-six-minute double-album, is its breadth. I don't mean this only lyrically, though any record that seeks to explain Spanish imperialists in Central America, the death of Montgomery Clift, American everymalls, nineteenth-century poker games, and the mean streets of Brixton screams ambition at every turn. Musically, the Clash use *London Calling* as a springboard away from punk in all directions—basic rock and roll, mainstream rock, reggae, New Orleans-style rhythm and blues, calypso, even big-production pop—although the punk ideal always holds sway. On *London Calling*, the Clash wanted to define an entire world just prior to blowing it up. Among double-albums, only *Exile on Main Street* covers more territory (you

20

Blonde on Blonde advocates can sit down now; in the next entry, I'll be arguing why that landmark double isn't even the best Dylan album).

Yet these nineteen songs cohere magnificently. One of the numbers, "Train in Vain," isn't even listed on the sleeve. In a scenario typical of the Clash's wary/incompetent approach to commercial necessities, the song no one could find turned out to be their first hit single in America. Some of the tracks meander a bit before they fade and some of the lyrics devolve into Dylan-derived dirty doggerel ("I believe in this and it's been tested by research/That he who fucks nuns will later join the church"), but aside from those few flaws to remind you that these guys aren't perfect—in fact, the group's inevitable self-destruction began almost immediately after the recording of *London Calling*—every moment on *London Calling* is as brazen and ultimately true as any rock and roll ever made.

London Calling earns these accolades not because the band so fervently believes what they are saying (hell, Styx and Kansas believe in the mush they emit), but because their music backs up even their wildest assertions. Whether juggling lyrics in the anthemic "Spanish Bombs," offering themselves as house band anywhere in the hilarious "Revolution Rock" (the same song in which Strummer claims, "I'm so pilled up that I r-r-rattle"), finding a middle ground between satire and declamation in "Lover's Rock," or damning American consumerism in "Lost in the Supermarket" and "Koka Kola," the music, recorded in appropriately dirty-clean fashion by producer Guy Stevens and engineer Bill Price, is terse and direct, as in-your-face as the Clash's previous records, but with more breathing room. The music for the songs that are most explicitly about the band—"Death or Glory" and "Four Horsemen"—is muscular and trustworthy enough to justify the bravado of the lyrics.

The Clash didn't stop here. Their next album, *Sandinista!*, was a sprawling mess, three albums of ooze that were even more wide-ranging, though not quite as consistent. Over repeated listenings, even the songs that were considered filler—dub versions of songs on the albums, children's-chorus versions of songs from earlier albums—gain weight. *Sandinista!* was the only studio triple-album in rock and roll worth the time or monetary investment.

One of my greatest thrills as a rock-and-roll fan was in 1982, at a stadium concert in Philadelphia, when the Clash (opening for the Who, in the first of what will no doubt be several dozen farewell tours) kicked off

21

their avalanche of a set with "London Calling" and Strummer punched the air to the beat. This commercially marginal band had gotten over to the masses without compromise. Ninety thousand hot, thirsty fans joined Strummer in the motion. I knew at the time that it was an empty gesture, and probably a manipulative one to boot. It didn't matter.

Number Eleven

Bob Dylan
Ten of Swords
Tarantula, 1985

Bootlegs are illegal, immoral, and too damned expensive. Although shoplifting them is morally defensible, you should not buy bootlegs. Yes, but this ten-album Bob Dylan box, pressed in Italy, is an instant classic. (You read that right: ten albums.) It is also everything *Biograph*, Columbia's five-LP above-the-counter compilation, should have been. Instead, *Biograph* was haphazard, unformed, and random, and we Dylan fans had no choice but to support the bootleggers. As bootlegs go, this is probably the greatest of them all: Nearly everything about it, from liner notes to sound quality, is professional quality (then again, how could the bootleggers come up with an album cover worse than the official-release *Knocked Out Loaded?*). And in terms of programming and sequencing, the mammoth collection devastates *Biograph*.

Side one of *Ten of Swords* was recorded in a hotel room in Minneapolis in 1961 and the set proceeds chronologically; side twenty slams shut with an awesome "Like a Rolling Stone" recorded at London's Royal Albert Hall with the Band in 1966. (Some argue that the legendary Royal Albert Hall bootleg was in fact recorded elsewhere in England, but let's save that argument for another book.) Between these bookends, one can hear Bob Dylan's evolution from a phenomenally gifted folk-blues master with Guthriesque pretensions to the greatest white American rocker of the decade. His first attempts at overt rock and roll here are tentative—a 1962 "Mixed-Up Confusion" is just what its title claims—but Dylan moves inexorably toward electric music; the outtakes from *Another Side of Bob Dylan* represent a rock-and-roll record without a band.

Everything here is marvelous, deserving of extended discussion, Dylan's voice sharpening, his arrangements gaining bark and bite, his subjects ironically getting more elliptical and specific at the same time. Among the most revealing cuts are excerpts from a Carnegie Hall taping intended for a live album but shelved at the last minute. The crucial number from this show is "Last Thoughts on Woody Guthrie," a staggering eight-minute poem recited at the speed of light that winds up to have next to nothing to do with the subject implied in the title. Dylan's subject throughout his classic period documented on *Ten of Swords* is his imagination and how far he can stretch it. Anyone who can conjure up both the hilarious, cocksure bedroom plea "If You Gotta Go, Go Now (Or Else You Gotta Stay All Night)" and "She's Your Lover Now," the nastiest song in the English language (although votes for "Positively Fourth Street" will be counted), is operating on an unchallengable level.

If there's anything wrong with *Ten of Swords* it's that it's not long enough. For example, only one side's worth of Dylan's 1966 studio date with the Band (from which "She's Your Lover Now" is drawn) has been unearthed. Perhaps it's greedy to want more of these grand excursions into the intersection between Chuck Berry and a roller coaster, but if desire is transcendent in a performer, it ought to be acceptable in a fan. Whatever the case, all is forgiven on the last two sides of the record, the complete electric half of the famed Royal Albert Hall (or wherever) gig. It's noisy, committed, offhand, unrelenting, even through the mean and unforgiving verbal battle Dylan shares with the "Judas!" yeller in the crowd. When he turns away from the microphone, it's impossible to tell whether Dylan is shouting "You're a fucking liar!" to the man in the crowd or "Play fucking loud!" to his friends onstage, before they all crash into "Like a Rolling Stone." Either way, it's the same message.

Embarrassed by such a set (Columbia briefly pulled advertising from *Rolling Stone* just because the magazine reported on it), Columbia eventually had to release *The Bootleg Series*, a three-CD set of outtakes that include many of these performances, though not nearly enough of them. More, though, are promised. And perhaps one day standing alongside irrefutably brilliant Dylan records already in the catalog (*Highway 61 Revisited, Blonde on Blonde, The Basement Tapes*, and *John Wesley Harding*, all from during or just after the period chronicled on *Ten of Swords*) will be collections that prove that Dylan's record company has a clue. But don't bet on it.

Number Twelve

Elvis Presley
*The Complete Burbank Sessions,
Vol. 1*
Audifon, no date listed, recorded
June 1968

It's May 1968, a heady moment for pop culture, though Elvis Presley is holed up in Hollywood. The thirty-three-year-old has cranked out three movies in the past year, just as he has for the past six. Presley (not merely his output) is dismissed by more than just the pop cognoscenti. His record-buying and movie-going fans have sensed that he has abandoned them, acting as if he can put out any old garbage and get away with it. He has all but stopped deigning to record anything aside from the compulsory soundtrack albums—and those particular products haven't spawned a Top Ten hit since 1963. Presley has recorded a bit of worthwhile music this year, but the relatively unadorned rock of "Guitar Man" and "U.S. Male" sounds like the luck of the draw.

A restless Tom Parker has finished scheming to get his boy back on television. It will be exceedingly polite: Christmas songs in a tuxedo. This arrangement sounds like death to Steve Binder, the relatively young producer NBC assigns to the show. Binder gets Elvis alone in his office and confronts him. (Well, almost alone. Ubiquitous chief crony Joe Esposito is at Elvis's side.) Binder suggests they take a walk outside. No bodyguards. Mid-afternoon, Presley, Binder, and Esposito walk along Sunset Strip and park themselves in front of the Classic Cat, a topless bar. They brace themselves for the onslaught. Nobody recognizes Elvis. The King shows off a bit, trying to gain the attention of passers-by, but he fails miserably and slumps back to Binder's office. Finally, Presley is aware of what will be at stake when the show airs December 3. The show belongs to Binder now, not Parker. The overfed carny will still battle Binder at every stop, but Elvis's support of Binder will irrevocably tip the scales.

First to go is the tuxedo, then all but one of the Christmas songs. Binder has gained Elvis's trust, a crucial ingredient to making the show believable. To help Presley feel even more comfortable, Binder starts hosting informal late-night sessions, either in his office or an empty, echoey soundstage. At the parties, Presley plays and jokes with old bandmates Scotty Moore and D.J. Fontana, and newer sidekicks Charlie Hodge, Lance Le Gault, and Alan Fortas.

These sessions go too well to revert to the normal variety-show format. There will be some of that—Binder has written a pair of ambitious production numbers he'll never abandon—but why not just let the cameras observe a few of these sessions and use them as blasts of fresh air between the more weighty numbers? Elvis, having a ball, whoops his approval.

So on June 29, 1968, Binder films Presley, Moore, Hodge, Fontana, and Fortas in a small stage set to look like a boxing ring without the ropes. Everyone wears beet-red Nehru suits except for Presley, whose black leather reflects the good humor of his comrades as well as the studio lights. The stage is too small to accommodate Fontana's drum kit, so he keeps time on a guitar case, with sticks, with brushes, with his hands. The jocular quintet sits in a circle, and they themselves are encircled by the audience. And for the first time in eight years, Elvis performs to a live audience.

On this must-own bootleg, you sense Elvis in the boxing ring, shining in black leather, hollering "Lawdy Miss Clawdy." The band stomps. Beaming, Scotty Moore tears from his Gibson the angular riffs he so badly wanted to use to enliven those bloated movie tunes; D.J. Fontana, the more pragmatic of the two old-timers, concentrates on deciphering the physics of making a guitar case sound like a full drum kit.

After trading guitars with Moore, Elvis races the compact unit through a steaming "Baby, What Do You Want Me to Do?" Elvis is playing lead electric guitar now. The tune peaks, then, on a whim, Elvis stops it because "There's something on my lip." It takes a second for the self-effacing joke to sink in, but the delayed roar is worth the wait. He loses the practiced sneer and laughs back, but intones, "I've got news for you, baby. I did twenty-nine pictures like that."

Charlie Hodge removes a few pieces of lint from Elvis's face and hands them to a swooning young fan. A raving "Trying to Get to You" leaves Elvis almost breathless, and he tears through "Baby, What Do You Want Me to Do?" again. This time it's a full version, complete with an extended lead-line introduction and break. The song gets faster, and Elvis briefly rises from his chair. He knows the segment is supposed to be relaxed, but he can't contain himself.

Feeling the end of the segment, Presley wants to kick his chair out of the ring and stand up straight. He wants a guitar strap so he can do this, but neither any of his bandmates nor any NBC stagehands can produce one. The hell with it, he thinks, propping his leg up on a chair, leaning his guitar on his leg, as Hodge precariously holds up a microphone boom stand so it can reach the upright singer.

"We wanna do one more song 'cause we've got another audience waiting to come in here," Elvis apologizes. The crowd sighs. Pretending to be powerless, he claims, "Man, I just work here." He appreciates the irony, smiling that he's back in control. "What a gig," Hodge chuckles.

For his last song in the boxing ring, Elvis picks Smiley Lewis's New Orleans standard, "One Night of Sin," a wondrously filthy blues that Elvis had cleaned up and recorded as "One Night with You" in 1958. Presley wiggles between the two versions, ostensibly singing the clean one, but appreciating that the malapropos politeness went out the door with "Jingle Bells" and the Christmas tux. He struggles to keep his guitar in control and stand up at the same time. He reverts from the wholesome line "The things that we two have planned/Could make my dreams come true" to the original "The things I did and I saw/Could make the earth stand still." The band notes the change and leans deeper into the song, especially Moore and a skeetering Fontana, thrilled to be finally playing the tune right. Elvis smiles back; the song carries them all home.

If you have to give RCA any business, opt for *The Complete Sun Sessions* and *Reconsider Baby*, Elvis's only blues albums.

Number Thirteen

The Beatles
Please Please Me
EMI, 1963

Every album the Beatles recorded prior to *Sgt. Pepper's Lonely Hearts Club Band* stands among rock and roll's greatest. *With the Beatles, A Hard Day's Night, Beatles for Sale, Help!, Rubber Soul, Revolver:* They're all explosions of energy and imagination strong enough to change the world, which the Beatles did over and over. But one of the records seems today the most mind-blowing in its expansion of what a pop record could do. One gives the most pleasure: the debut album, *Please Please Me.* It's innocent, it smiles too much, and it doesn't have a fraction of the sophistication that John, Paul, George, and Ringo would develop less than a year after recording it, but it stands out as the most lovable of Beatles records. (If you're wondering, I think *Sgt. Pepper* is a pretentious mess and a bad influence on rock and roll in general, although I do enjoy its audacity and its inside jokes.) Much ink has been wasted over claims of how later albums like *The White Album* and *Abbey Road* stretched rock and roll's boundaries, but no rock-band record of the sixties changed the rules so much as *Please Please Me.*

Please Please Me explodes to life with "I Saw Her Standing There," a fiery rocker built on Ringo's surprising drum fills and a guitar solo from George that touched on Chuck Berry and Scotty Moore, but then spiraled up to uncharted territory. The title track, all harmonica and harmonies, is far more unclean-minded than its bright exterior, and "There's a Place" and the exuberant version of the Isley Brothers' "Twist and Shout" extended listeners' ideas of . . .

Wait a minute. This song-by-song stuff is absurd; anyone reading this book already knows these songs like they were relatives. So here's the real point: As Mark Shipper has suggested, the idea behind the Beatles' debut album was to change the face of pop music forever, and that is but one of its achievements. Listen to *Please Please Me* away from all this foolishness about ranking and making the relative case for a Beatles album. Instead, imagine a world in which *Please Please Me* never existed. Your affection for the group and the changes it wrought will increase exponentially.

Number Fourteen

Bruce Springsteen
Nebraska
Columbia, 1982

Why *Nebraska?*

Bruce Springsteen is the most gifted rocker of his generation. Onstage with his since-dismissed E Street Band, he was the king of live rock and roll in the seventies and eighties. Still, some of his records (and some tours) have lasted better than others. *The Saint, the Incident, and the Main Point,* a bootleg of a live show in Pennsylvania in early 1975, chronicles one of the finest of his pre-*Born to Run* performances definitively. But *Born to Run* these days comes across as overblown, except for "Thunder Road" and the title track, which seems to have gained considerable resonance and weight over the years. The same can't be said for a cut like "Jungleland," which for all its power probably belongs in a theatrical production, mostly for the way Springsteen sang it. Throughout *Born to Run* and much of his next album, *Darkness on the Edge of Town* (a much tighter batch of songs and performances), Springsteen sang with an exaggeratedly low voice, perhaps in an attempt to sound tougher. He sang all those songs better live then, away from such overdeliberative studio techniques, and he sings them even better now as the affectations in his voice have dissipated.

Springsteen's eighties work seems more likely to sound fresh at the turn of the century. *The River* finally gave voice to all the sundry characters in Springsteen's mind, *Born in the U.S.A.* expanded both his interests and his abilities, and *Tunnel of Love* held the deliberations of a grown man who had clearly thought a great deal about how to streamline his music, his ideas, and his life. That Springsteen's crown has chipped considerably since then is merely another example of how we buy records by great artists, not great human beings. He doesn't record nearly as much as Prince, his only platinum peer (and someone who is probably even stranger than the Boss), but his batting average is just as high.

But I keep coming back to *Nebraska*. I return to its offhand pronouncements, its specificity of musical, lyrical, and emotional detail, its remarkable pessimism, and its refusal to romanticize that pessimism. The last number on this solo acoustic album is "Reason to Believe," a series of reasons why belief is the most bewildering joke of all in this life. Fans and critics went into contortions trying to explain why that fatalistic tune was in fact some sort of affirmation (Springsteen's earlier work encouraged them to make such judgments), which said more about the emptiness in the lives of the fans and critics than in Springsteen's.

I love *Nebraska* for its unconventionality, its humor, its obsessiveness, and its refusal to succumb to rock conventions. *Nebraska* is a once-in-a-lifetime album, and not only because Springsteen would have to sell his fourteen-million-dollar house and get a real job if he kept putting out desolate records with no hit singles. *Nebraska* is as close as Springsteen will ever get to blues feeling, if not blues form. (Steel Mill was bad enough, thank you.) Most of these songs take place on some unknown highway at some ungodly hour, a lonely narrator begging for some connection to something, be it a woman, a job, a radio disc jockey, or a half-forgotten family.

Nebraska, as much as *Astral Weeks*, is a record about being alone, about being desperate, about being brave enough to admit that there's no easy cure for desperation. It's an idea Springsteen would pick up on for "Dancing in the Dark" and most of *Tunnel of Love*, but only on *Nebraska* does rock and roll's great uplifter have the guts to admit that for some people the world may never be a friendly place.

Number Fifteen

The Jimi Hendrix Experience
Radio One
Rykodisc, 1988

If Jimi Hendrix were still alive, he probably wouldn't have released as many albums as have appeared since his death. It seems that every time the poor guy plugged in, someone with a tape recorder was lurking in the shadows. The records over which Hendrix had some control while he was alive—*Are You Experienced?*, *Axis: Bold as Love*, *Electric Ladyland*, and *Band of Gypsies*—are all precise, dramatic sets in which the visionary guitarist and bandleader took care with his every nuance. Hendrix was something of a control freak—why else would he build his own studio?—and that makes the posthumous packages especially distressing.

Yet the Hendrix record that seems truest to the artist was released eighteen years after he died, on a record label he'd never heard of: *Radio One*, the second of Rykodisc's superb Hendrix reissues. *Radio One* is a collection of seventeen tracks recorded for various BBC radio shows in 1967, and it is the purest Hendrix disc available. Since he's in someone else's studio, forced to go in and out swiftly, there are minimal effects here. This is the most unencumbered Jimi Hendrix Experience record imaginable: Hendrix, bassist Noel Redding, and drummer Mitch Mitchell simply plug in and burn. There are incredible constraints placed on this occasionally free-form unit; because no song here lasts longer than five-and-one-half minutes, the group's trademark improvisations have to take place within the context of an existing song.

Those whose version of Hendrix is heavy on the jazz-cat side might resent this, but for those of us who love Hendrix for his ability to transcend rock-and-roll form without straying from its blues base, this is a godsend. This is the clearest, most song-oriented of all Hendrix's sundry albums, and only *Electric Ladyland* coheres better as a unified work.

From the hilarious "Radio One Theme" to a thundering take on Curtis Knight's "Drivin' South," from the lysergic recasting of the Beatles' "Day Tripper" to expansive-in-context versions of songs that would wind up on the three Experience albums, Hendrix takes on the whole of his repertoire and technique. Not bad for a Saturday-morning radio show.

Number Sixteen

Lonnie Mack
The Wham! of That Memphis Man
Fraternity, 1964

The first of the guitar-hero records is also one of the best. And for perhaps the last time, the singing on such a disc is worthy of the guitar histrionics. Lonnie Mack bent, stroked, and modified the sound of six strings in ways that baffled his contemporaries and served as a guide to future players. Eric Clapton's later take on Bobby Bland's "Farther on Down the Road" outright swipes the version of the standard which Clapton first heard on this album.

But Mack is more than just an axe murderer. His singing is sure, full of knowing nuance, and soulful—his screams transform "Why" from an above-par breakup ballad into a run of psychic terror—and his brash arrangements insure that *Wham!* remains a showcase for songs, not a platform for showing off. Although Mack is a fine writer, the accent here is on songs written by others. Chuck Berry's "Memphis" (Mack's first single and an instrumental chart smash) and Dale Hawkins's "Suzie Q" aren't radically reworked, but Mack imprints both numbers with enough spiraling, sputtering guitar to distinguish them from their original incarnations.

Mack envelops himself in the ballads; "Where There's a Will There's a Way" and the climactic "Why" demonstrate his measured, thoughtful vocal eruptions to best effect. Still, it is Mack's guitar playing that made his career and remains his most enduring legacy. He played fast and he played lots of notes, yet on *Wham!* he never went on too long or ground his gears by squeezing too much into a break. Mack, who produced this album, has never been given credit for the dignified understatement he brought to his workouts. In the mid-eighties he was rediscovered, thanks to Stevie Ray Vaughan and the good folks at Alligator Records, and thanks to reissue specialists *The Wham! of That Memphis Man* started to get some of the attention it deserved.

Number Seventeen

Dusty Springfield
Dusty in Memphis
Atlantic, 1968

In 1967 Aretha Franklin moved from Columbia to Atlantic and swiftly advanced from a woman with a great set of pipes who didn't have a clue what to do with them to the greatest singer of her time. Others got the message and record companies were soon sending washed-up female singers down south by the planeload, figuring that the proximity to the studios used by Atlantic and its associate Stax label would be useful.

The most successful of these reclamation projects was also one of the most unlikely. Dusty Springfield was a British pop singer who was rather adept at fluff with a hint of Motown-style soul ("I Only Want to Be With You," etc.), but she did not suggest in her monochromatic performances that she had anything more substantial in her. Jerry Wexler of Atlantic Records sensed otherwise and brought Springfield to American Studios in Memphis.

Although much has been written about Springfield's surprising ability to accommodate new forms, it's worth noting that the session players at American were thrilled to have an opportunity to stretch out themselves. Guitarist Reggie Young, bassist Tommy Cogbill, keyboard players Bobby Emmons and Bobby Wood, and drummer Gene Christian had played on all sorts of great records, but not the sort of sophisticated pop/soul Wexler and coproducers Tom Dowd and Arif Mardin had in mind. The singer brought a lot to *Dusty in Memphis*, but, just as important, the band was ready to accept it and respond to it.

The other keys to the masterfulness of this record are Arif Mardin's string arrangements and the background vocals by the Sweet Inspirations. Strings and voices swirl around Springfield in the wise "Son of a Preacher Man," the devastated "I Don't Want to Hear It Anymore," and the somewhere-in-between "Don't Forget About Me." The most impressive cut is the smoldering "Breakfast in Bed," a tale of hopeless love and longing mirrored perfectly in Cogbill's quiet, empathetic bass and the entire rising arrangement. The band plays so persuasively and Springfield sings with such intensity it's easy to believe that heartbreak might not be irrevocable anymore.

Springfield wasn't a singer of Aretha's caliber, she wasn't even aiming that high, but *Dusty in Memphis* was so extraordinary and unforeseen that such comparisons were inevitable.

Number Eighteen

Various Performers
1000 Volts of Stax: Rare and Unissued Tracks from the Golden Era of Soul
Ace, 1991

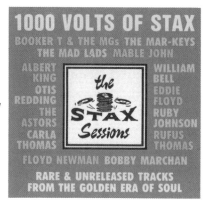

Twenty-five years after the company's heyday, it still seems like the treasure chest that is the Stax Records catalog might be bottomless. The Memphis country-soul label, founded in 1959, grabbed the front-running baton from its crosstown competition Sun and by the early Sixties had become the most important of all American independent labels. Stax Records, and its Volt subsidiary, gave voice to all sorts of sounds and ideas that even inspired similar-minded labels like Motown had sidestepped.

Stax yielded some great stars—the singers Eddie Floyd and Carla Thomas, as well as the unmatchable accompanists Booker T. Jones, Steve Cropper, Donald Dunn, and Al Jackson—but Stax wasn't just about its Otis Reddings and Sam and Daves, its major stars. More than any of the other groundbreaking Sixties labels, Stax headquarters at 926 McLemore Avenue was truly a place where producers, performers, and writers truly worked as a unit, not as individuals, at least as far as the finished product was concerned. The Atlantic sales representatives who promoted Stax singles may have preferred more Otis Redding records and less Mable John (Little Willie John's little sister, best-known in soul-collector circles for the dark "Don't Hit Me No More"), but in the studio there was only one tier for these masters of restrained anarchy.

Stax enjoyed an astonishing batting average, as evidenced by the essential *The Complete Stax-Volt Singles, 1959–1968*, and several other brilliant repackagings, among them the little-known but marvelous *1000 Volts of Stax: Rare and Unreleased Tracks from the Golden Era of Soul*. Put out by the exemplary British reissue label Ace, *1000 Volts of Stax* is a teaser for the hidden tapes in Stax's vaults, now run by the Fantasy label.

1000 Volts of Stax doesn't include any hit versions of songs (notable alternate takes here include Rufus Thomas barking through "Walking the Dog" and Eddie Floyd in a delirious live version of "Knock on Wood"); even more than the *Singles* box, it showcases how much the label's less-known recordings have to offer. Plus, you get to hear Otis Redding sing Sam Cooke's "Cupid." Sometimes researchers have the most fun. This time we can all join in.

Number Nineteen

Carl Perkins
The Classic Carl Perkins
Bear Family, 1990

"They took a light from a honky-tonk/Put the gleam in your eye," Carl Perkins howls on "Honky Tonk Gal," one of his many amazing performances on *The Classic Carl Perkins,* a stellar five-CD boxed set that includes all his recordings for Sun Records and those shortly thereafter. With such a line, Perkins neatly encapsulates rockabilly's concerns and fears.

Rockabilly, that reckless, primal thrash of honky-tonk country-and-western, is all about conflict—between rural and urban, between barroom adventure and home comfort, between the headfirst sin of Saturday nights and the heartfelt repentance of Sunday mornings. The honky-tonk gal Perkins adores is both his joy (she's hot stuff and knows it) and his pain (she's no longer a demure housewife). She's the conflict of rockabilly personified.

Perkins treats this dilemma the way any self-respecting rockabilly cat would: He blazes out fiery riffs and drives through the quandary in fifth gear. He'll deal with the consequences of his rampage tomorrow. Even lost in the thrill of taking his Gibson guitar for an unexpected joyride, he knows that somewhere down the road there will be a price to pay. Rockabilly is about release, but its release always has limits—that's the form's country birthright.

That's also what makes Perkins, a pure rockabilly performer then and always, different from Elvis Presley or Roy Orbison, rockabilly cats who expanded into straight pop and, in doing so, uprooted themselves. "You could never take the country out of Perkins," veteran Sun-reissue compiler Colin Escott wrote in one of his many expert liner-note essays, pinpointing what set Perkins apart from Presley and what prevented him from achieving Elvis-like success. Presley, for all his indisputable greatness, sold out for pop success in every way imaginable. Perkins, even in his most banal countrypolitan settings, never surrendered.

This massive set has no fluff. Perkins's gracious, quavering tenor carries some magnificent country ballads; among the most noteworthy are "Turn Around," his first professional recording, and "Let the Jukebox Keep on Playing," the most understated expression of honky-tonk regret and paralysis in post-Hank Williams country music. But Perkins's meat is his rockabilly, "Blue Suede Shoes" and all that, in which he repeatedly drives full speed to the edge of his world, leans over the cliff to enjoy the view for a brief second, and then, as he knows he must, pulls back and carefully heads home.

"Rockabilly sure takes me over the edge," top Stray Cat Brian Setzer countered when I threw that idea at him a few years ago. "It's the most menacing music. Heavy metal is kid's stuff compared to it." Yes, but Setzer and the many legions who adopted pompadours in the late seventies discovered the music and the accoutrements, not the culture. It's no accident that most of the rockabilly revivalists came from northern urban areas. To them, rockabilly is Gene Vincent's leer and Eddie Cochran's shake without regard for the honky-tonk imperatives behind them. The Stray Cats, since reduced to beer commercials, can afford to shoot over the edge; Perkins and his contemporaries, who didn't have the luxury of growing up in a society that had already been liberated by rock and roll, had no such romantic alternative.

Yet on "Dixie Fried," his greatest uptempo composition, Perkins comes as close as any rockabilly performer to going over the edge and living to tell about it. His guitar flashes like the barroom-fight switchblades his tale chronicles; his voice dances with the wobbly exuberance of his brazen, drunken protagonist. "Let's all get Dixie fried!" he screams, shattering any pretensions to caution, or civilized behavior. The violence escalates and the song smashes to its head-on conclusion, not with the law, but with the inevitable. Perkins may have the gleam of the honky-tonk in his eye, but his eye is fixed on home, where he prays his honky-tonk gal has returned.

Number Twenty

Creedence Clearwater Revival
Willie and the Poor Boys
Fantasy, 1969

America's greatest rock-and-roll band? You bet.

At a time when stretching out was all the rage, John Fogerty opted for a defiant concision that makes his band's music timeless when much of the trendier material from the late sixties now sounds silly. What turned into Creedence Clearwater Revival formed in El Cerrito, California, in the early sixties, and the lack of privileged status enjoyed by Fogerty, his brother Tom, Doug Clifford, and Stu Cook, at least in comparison to their contemporaries, always stayed with them. Wordiness and extended jams were rarely a part of Creedence Clearwater Revival's mix: John Fogerty, who led the band with his singing, songwriting, lead guitar playing, arranging, and producing, opted for direct expression nearly every time. John had grown up on lanky rockabilly records from Memphis and loping rhythm-and-blues records from New Orleans—he admired the compression in those cuts and sought to say what needed to be said plainly and then move on. He didn't have time for bullshit, and he assumed that his audience didn't either.

Although tautness was a virtue in John Fogerty's heart and mind, he wasn't afraid to speak metaphorically. In songs like "Who'll Stop the Rain?", "Proud Mary," and "Run Through the Jungle," among many other hits, he opted for a grand generality. As long as he worked in the constraints of potential hit singles, Fogerty could thrive (as soon as the members of Creedence Clearwater Revival opted for extended jams on record, the group began to shatter). "I wrote a song for everyone," Fogerty sang. That was his most wide-eyed dream, and the one he could achieve only by speaking from heart to heart. His rough voice was nobody's idea of pretty, but his gruff, resilient tenor worked because of its total confidence and lack of pretension. Not only did Creedence Clearwater Revival have hit singles, but it had two-sided hit singles, something rare in the time and virtually unknown in these make-the-consumer-buy-as-many-items-as-possible times; that's how committed Fogerty was to his conversational method.

Willie and the Poor Boys is one of Creedence Clearwater Revival's two beginning-to-end great records, and it's greater than *Green River* because it boasts the tumultuous rocker "Fortunate Son," an angry song in the midst of love-and-peace-man times and a cry for truth that hasn't dated at all, mostly because its ferocious guitars and drums never forgot that they were in service of the song. (Alas, the song seems even more relevant today.) But *Willie and the Poor Boys* offered far more than just one great single. "It Came Out of the Sky" is a rockabilly raver about a flying saucer that falls to earth in which Fogerty delicately skewers all those who try to capitalize on it ("Ronnie the Popular said it was a communist plot," he sings, referring to an opportunistic incompetent who at that time controlled only one state) and rolls over them all with his rhythm-based lead lines. *Willie and the Poor Boys* runs through remarkably diverse genres for a record by a "rock" band: "Cotton Fields" and "Don't Look Now" are straight country, "Poorboy Shuffle" stands somewhere between skiffle and Louisiana blues, "Feelin' Blue" is a choogling swamp blues, "Effigy" is one of Fogerty's trademark apocalyptic tunes and perhaps his most ominous.

It makes sense that Fogerty climaxed *Willie and the Poor Boys* with "Effigy," its most foreboding tune, because that's what was in his deepest heart. In "Effigy" we don't find out exactly what's wrong, but we can tell that something is deeply amiss. John Fogerty wrote rock-and-roll songs in Creedence Clearwater Revival for the thrill of being in a rock-and-roll band, but also because he saw horror around him—even in comeback mode Fogerty is rock's most fatalistic major songwriter—and he wanted to find a way to understand it, maybe even accept it. And if he got that far, he said through his songs, he would drop some clues along the way for us. He never got that far, but his adventures remain among rock and roll's most daring.

43

Number Twenty-One

Little Richard
The Specialty Sessions
Ace/Specialty, 1989

"You ain't never gave me nuthin'!" Little Richard shouted at the Grammy Awards Ceremonies a few years back, and the record-industry crowd in the auditorium laughed at him. For more than thirty years, Richard has been rock and roll's court jester, someone who knows he is funny and can amuse anyone in any way he chooses. But Richard—whose talent is nothing to laugh at—was not joking, which made the moment that much more poignant.

Because Richard encourages the industry to laugh at him (and, let's face it, because of the color of his skin), he has never gotten what he deserves in terms of respect, money, or credit. It's easy to focus on his hair, his mugging for the camera, and the way he shouts "Wooooo!" Aside from those who worked out of Sun Records, Little Richard is the most important midwife to the birth of rock and roll. Already a seasoned rhythm-and-blues singer when he arrived at Specialty Records, Richard discovered a revved-up version of uptempo New Orleans-style rhythm-and-blues and found a way to put across his most randy ideas ("I saw Uncle John with Bald-Headed Sally/He saw Aunt Mary comin' and he ducked back in the alley"; "I'm gonna ring your door 'til I break your bell") so quickly and ostensibly randomly that he would not earn widespread denunciation. More so than any of the other originators of rock and roll, Richard thought of himself as a freak, different from the mainstream. But Richard reveled in his status; he screamed profound nonsense lines like "Wop Bop a-Loo Bop a-Lop Bam Boom" and "Bama Lama Lama Loo" and in every way did his utmost to skirt issues of conformity.

Although Richard has recorded consistently since the early fifties, his greatest records remain those cut for the Specialty label in the late fifties.

44

Nothing he recorded during his brief tenure at Art Rupe's company is less than excellent, as evidenced on these two complementary box sets: The three-CD Specialty version includes at least one version of every song he cut there, while the six-disc import set from Ace is rich in alternate takes, usually three or four per song. What's most impressive about these sets is their consistent energy. Richard pinned himself in fifth gear the moment he arrived at Specialty and stayed up there until he left in one of his periodic abandonments of worldly music. The major hits—"Tutti Frutti," "Long Tall Sally," "Jenny Jenny," "Keep A Knockin'," "Good Golly Miss Molly," and many more—defined an individual approach to rock and roll: horns rolling over second-line rhythms, stacatto piano lines punctuating the spry arrangement, and Richard's alert, otherworldly voice on top, shouting and overmodulating. Some have argued that Little Richard is not a major artist because he never surpassed his original sides, but the audacity and hysteria of these sides have never been equaled by anyone, not just Richard. And he still hasn't gotten paid.

Number Twenty-Two

Derek and the Dominoes
Layla and Other Assorted Love Songs
RSO, 1970

Nowadays, Eric Clapton is the most overrated guitarist in the history of rock and roll—what else can you say about someone who has inspired "CLAPTON IS GOD" graffiti?—but he is also one of the most impressive of all six-string masters. Few white players have his understanding, his full internalization, of the blues; few players of any instrument anywhere—including singers—are capable of wrenching so many different emotions in so many non-manipulative fashions. The problem is that Clapton doesn't want to anymore. He feels he's already "done his bit," as the former Johnny Rotten says of his past nowadays. Clapton makes bland pop records and hangs out with Phil Collins; among non-dead rockers, he is a waste of talent second only to Rod Stewart. Once in a while, like on mid-eighties gigs with Carl Perkins and Chuck Berry, or even (horror of horrors) when admitted alcoholic Clapton recorded a beer jingle, he turns on the juice. Most of the time he can't be bothered.

It wasn't always this way. Around 1970, Clapton was among the most unrequited of rockers. He was already a superstar from his days with the ill-fated supergroup Blind Faith and the ill-conceived power trio Cream, and he wanted to pump down the volume but still find edgy sounds. He performed as a sideman for Delaney and Bonnie, and immersed himself in soul music. He surrounded himself with American musicians from Delaney and Bonnie's troupe who had no use for the excesses of Cream, and pared down. Clapton, keyboard player Bobby Whitlock, bassist Carl Radle, and drummer Jim Gordon called themselves Derek and the Dominoes, ensconced themselves in Miami, and wrote and recorded the most direct album of Clapton's career.

Clapton is striving throughout the seventy-seven minutes of *Layla and*

Other Assorted Love Songs, trying to get his guitar to talk right, trying to get his voice right, trying to ease his worried mind, trying to keep trying. Clapton's personal life was a wreck when he cut this album (drugs, barbed romance, more drugs) and perhaps that's why he found solace in the cathartic blues and blues-derived cuts on this record. "I don't wanna fade away" he and Whitlock sing like Sam and Dave in "Bell Bottom Blues," and that was precisely Clapton's worry—that he didn't matter emotionally or musically. But Clapton and company (all of whom had their own megaproblems at the time as well) stirred through songs they loved (Chuck Willis's resigned "It's Too Late," Jimi Hendrix's ominous "Little Wing," and a pair of blues standards) as well as songs of their own making that lived up to those of their forbears. *Layla and Other Assorted Love Songs* is an album about desperately trying to find order in a world as disordered as any imaginable.

Extraordinarily instinctive vocal and instrumental arrangements dominate the record, especially on the titanic "Layla," the only lengthy rock-radio standard that still stands up twenty years later as something other than nostalgia. Any rock-and-roll fan knows the song, from the slashing dual-guitar (or is that duel-guitar?) introduction of Clapton and guest Duane Allman to the extended coda that seems the aural embodiment of pian. "Layla" is a song that summons up Robert Johnson and then finds a way to get darker, which is an achievement in itself. "Layla," a raw tale of love as unrequited as any in art, is as naked as any song in rock and roll, as exposed as anything Clapton ever recorded. No wonder he had to pull back afterward.

Number Twenty-Three

Ray Charles
Ray Charles Live
Atlantic, 1973

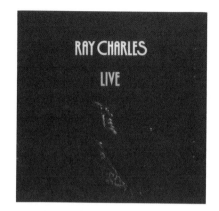

Although I pledge my love to the album listed above, fairness dictates that I alert you to the existence of *The Birth of Soul: The Complete Atlantic Rhythm and Blues Sessions, 1952–1959*. It's a three-CD set that nearly lives up to the definitiveness implied by its title. Charles churched the blues. Sorry about the neologism but his achievement is so monumental that existing language cannot contain it. Charles claims that "What'd I Say," the definitive rhythm-and-blues song, was improvised and we should take him at his word, since the number seems sprung from some collective cultural unconscious, like Marvin Gaye's version of "I Heard It Through the Grapevine" or Lightnin' Hopkins's "Death Bells." Amazingly, Charles expanded on his original achievements, and although an argument can be made for the objective superiority of his studio work, like most great entertainers Charles saved something extra for his live shows.

Assembled from two previously released live sets (1958's *Ray Charles at Newport*, which shocked the stodgy crowd, and *Ray Charles in Person*, cut in Atlanta a year later) and put out long after Charles abandoned Atlantic for ABC/Paramount, this double-album offers up the Genius as an onstage hurricane, unstoppable, uprooting all in his path, whether he wants to "Drown in My Own Tears" or praise the nighttime as "The Right Time" with head Raylette and the queen of call and response, Marjorie Hendricks. Charles's piano playing, especially at Newport, is percussive and melodic at once; on "I Got a Woman" he directs both the horns and the drums with rhythmic asides. There are some soft spots—the Latin-tinged "In a Little Spanish Town" and the cha-cha "Frenesi" now come across as arcane period pieces—but even the lesser tunes are pushed across by a man and band at their peaks. Drummers Richie Goldberg and Teagle Fleming and tenor saxophonist David "Fathead" Newman are especially noteworthy; the beat holds up the piano, and Newman's frantic solos, especially on "Blues Waltz," slice through the beat. Charles presides above it all, never wavering, emphatic, decisive. Charles has become as stolid and officially venerated as any national monument, but this collection reminds us what a rule breaker he once was. Plus, it ends with "What'd I Say."

Number Twenty-Four

Bo Diddley
Bo Diddley's Beach Party
Chess, 1963

I know that Ellis McDaniel has been the subject of some fine compilations (put down this book and buy *The Chess Box* immediately), but I want to celebrate this album's awesome grunge.

Forget *The Kingsmen on Campus*, forget *Nuggets*. This live album is the most delightfully primitive rock-and-roll album ever. Recorded during two hot nights in July 1963 at the Beach Club in Myrtle Beach, South Carolina, *Bo Diddley's Beach Party* is Bo at his most brazen and caustic, even if there are only Caucasian faces on the cover of this record. The sound quality lies somewhere below horrible, with vocals and instruments sliding in and out of earshot; even Diddley's legendary rectangular guitar settles into the murk from time to time.

But what never sinks from center stage is Bo Diddley's barbed-wire presence. He never ventures from his unshakable boasts—"Bo Diddley Is a Gunslinger," "Hey Bo Diddley," "Bo Diddley's Dog," and "Bo's Waltz" suggest the extent of his interests. (No doubt that MCA, which owns the Chess catalog, is sitting on a tape of "Bo Diddley Is God.") Bo is in love with himself, all right, but he is more in love with music. Specifically, he's enamored of the electrified shave-and-a-haircut/two-bits stomp that he gave rock and roll and which subsequently has been picked up by everyone from Buddy Holly to Chrissie Hynde. Ben Vaughn cut a tune to Bo's beat called "I'm Not Bo Diddley." No one argued.

So all here reduces to beat. "What's buggin' you?" he asks as a throwaway deep into Side Two. "Well, knock it off."

Amusing consumer note: Long out of print, *Bo Diddley's Beach Party* was recently reissued in Japan, including a riotous lyric sheet that translates the line "Bo Diddley at the O.K. Corral" as "My poor Lily and ol' Greg Morell." Ah, Dada.

Number Twenty-Five

Various Performers
Greatest Rap Hits, Vol. 2
Sugarhill, 1981

Before it became the soundtrack for fast-food commercials, rap was the sound of a brash subculture. The leading independent labels at the beginning were Tommy Boy, who put out the early records by Afrika Bambaataa and Soul Sonic Force, and Sugarhill Records, owned by Sylvia Robinson (half of the old Mickey and Sylvia "Love Is Strange" duo), who put out damn near everything else. Sugarhill had the first rap smash—the Sugarhill Gang's epic "Rapper's Delight"—and attracted some of the best groups and session players. Their greatest band was Grandmaster Flash and the Furious Five, who provide three of this record's six songs, all of the best. The grand conclusion of this compilation, and arguably hip hop's greatest hit, is from Grandmaster Flash and the Furious Five, a single called "The Adventures of Grandmaster Flash on the Wheels of Steel."

As digital sampling becomes more and more pervasive as a recording technique in pop, the belief that anything is possible in a studio nowadays is also on the rise. But "Wheels of Steel" took the cut-and-paste-sound approach used covertly on many records today (hello, Vanilla Ice) and the scavenging of other songs as its very subject. (Wheels of steel are turntables.) The number asks: How smart can you steal? How slick can you mix? This technical apex of one of rap's leading disc-spinners is tremendously influential—many of today's dance-music and rock productions are unimaginable without it.

Flash started as a South Bronx dance-hall disc jockey whose trademark was taking his favorite rock and rap songs and repeating their hottest elements for heightened effect. "Wheels of Steel" was a solo shot by Flash designed to show off the wizardry that knocked 'em out live. After a stuttering intro, Flash lets Blondie's "Rapture," Chic's "Good Times," and Queen's "Another One Bites the Dust," as well as snippets from earlier Flash/Five singles glide in and slam out of the unwavering beat. These songs of different tempos all fit without being forced. Spoken sections, boasts, and song apexes are finely woven into an amazingly seamless whole. Before the serrated-edged righteousness of "The Message" and "White Lines (Don't Don't Do It)" turned attention to rapper and writer Melle Mel, the group was a showcase for Flash. This is why.

Number Twenty-Six

Neil Young
Tonight's the Night
Reprise, 1975

In the liner notes to his brilliant and slightly misleading collection *Decade*, Neil Young wrote about his massive hit single "Heart of Gold": "This song put me in the middle of the road. Travelling there soon became a bore so I headed for the ditch. A rougher ride but I saw more interesting people there." That's his career in a nutshell. Bravely, he threw away a certain career as a folk-rock/country-rock heartthrob for a more treacherous mixture of hard rock and hard turns. On the other hand, would you want to hang out with James Taylor? David Crosby?

Young drags his fans through the wilderness sometimes for years between good albums (as I write this, Young has released five supportable LPs in a row, an all-time record for him), but that's primarily because he expects his legions to be as restless as he. His first turnaround, and still his most radical, was the aforementioned move to the ditch after *Harvest.* Young recorded *Tonight's the Night* in 1973, and it took him nearly two years (or so the legend goes) to talk Warner Brothers into releasing the harsh, off-kilter work that alienated fans of "Heart of Gold" as surely as Sly and the Family Stone's *There's a Riot Goin' On* scared off buyers of their earlier, lighter hits. All Young had to do was plug in his electric guitar, play his modal, minor-key solos, and watch 'em scatter.

As with some other major Young albums (*Rust Never Sleeps, Freedom*), two versions of one song on *Tonight's the Night* bookend the record. The take of the title track that starts the record is loose, the slightly longer one that ends it is fundamentally dissolute. The song, as well as a few others on the record, takes on the deaths of two people close to Young in the early seventies, both due to heroin. Young's singing is wobbly, his accompaniment is bloody, everybody's prospects seem bleak.

54

Young has acknowledged that the band was high when they cut *Tonight's the Night*, an irony that emphasizes Young's closeness to his material. But *Tonight's the Night* isn't about drugs, in spite of songs like "Tired Eyes" that explicitly tackle the horrors of dealing and shooting up; it's about determination. Young sounds out of it throughout this record—"Speakin' Out," a blues based on Dylan's "Pledging My Time," is full of random details that add up to all-encompassing weirdness—more specifically, he sounds like he's coming out of a dream. *Tonight's the Night* is a belated trip to reality, and it's hard to blame the recovering Young for not liking what he saw there.

Number Twenty-Seven

Marvin Gaye
What's Going On/Let's Get It On
Motown, 1971/1973

Motown's CD reissue campaign has been a long fizz for many of its artists, and even though this compact disc sounds remastered from an LP-equalized tape and is something of a sonic dud, this is indispensable. All the contradictions of forward-thinking African-American pop in the early seventies assert themselves on this CD-only pairing of Marvin Gaye's two most exceptional original-release albums. *What's Going On* is one of the early-seventies LPs that expanded the vernacular of Motown pop, and its follow-up *Let's Get It On* articulated love and lust in ways that presented sex as what it is for adults, a temporary escape from the world. Not until Prince's "1999" (the single, not the album) did someone articulate this dichotomy between social awareness and personal necessities more succinctly.

Gaye had already traveled a long way when he arrived at these triumphs. After his tutelage under Harvey Fuqua in a late permutation of the Moonglows, he moved to Motown and the tutelage of Berry Gordy, married the boss's sister, and worked as a session drummer and percussionist until he got his chance to shine in the spotlight. His first pair of singles, "Stubborn Kind of Fellow" and "Hitch Hike," weren't smashes, but they did set the pattern for the major hits to follow: his willful yet smooth voice atop a tale of generalized spiritual/romantic yearning. By the end of the sixties, he had transcended Motown form, recording the tumultuous "I Heard It Through the Grapevine" (a record whose ramifications deserve their own book) and several dozen duets with Tammi Terrell that remain the liveliest, most hopeful series of tales celebrating romantic fidelity ever.

But Gaye wanted more. *What's Going On* towered over most soul albums, even the better ones, in that it was a conceptual work with musical and lyrical themes throughout; as far as concept went, it owed far more to *Tommy* than any record released by Motown. Gaye's tone on the record was anguished but searching, through songs about war, pollution, God, and, most of all, himself. The seven-minutes-and-thirty-one-seconds "Right On" broke rules about what could happen on a soul record and not just because it sported a flute solo; throughout *What's Going On,* Gaye was experimenting, trying to discover new ways to sing, emote, project. A case can be made that "Inner City Blues (Make Me Wanna Holler)" revealed nothing so much as Gaye's distance from the subject, but since the whole record is about wanting to connect, it's likely that Gaye had some sense of his predicament.

Connecting was also the key to *Let's Get It On,* which was a bit more conventional musically (soul crossing into mild funk) and much more focused lyrically. The record is about loneliness, about ego, about all that goes into someone's mind when he or she is trying to make another person matter. *Let's Get It On* takes place in a bedroom, but it's about more than the act itself. As much as *What's Going On,* the album is about fitting into a perfect community. It's impossible to choose *What's Going On* over *Let's Get It On* or vice versa. For once, thanks to the marketing folks at Motown for making this one easy.

Number Twenty-Eight

The Costello Show (Featuring
Elvis Costello)
King of America
Columbia, 1986

In late 1977, twenty-two-year-old British songwriter/singer Elvis Costello played his first dates in America. Those early performances were short and furious: "Revenge and guilt," he told early interviewers who asked his motives. The shows climaxed with the guitarist and his band, the Attractions, drenching their audiences in waves of feedback as they vacated the stage. "I'm not angry," Costello sang on his debut album, *My Aim Is True*. The irony couldn't have been more pronounced.

The mainstream American pop audience first heard Costello during a *Saturday Night Live* appearance in which he halted a familiar song and ordered the Attractions to start "Radio Radio," a damnation of American radio that helped insure his long-time blackballing from it. The pair of albums that followed, the punk-inspired *This Year's Model* and pop deconstruction *Armed Forces*, established Costello as a resourceful songwriter who dissected domestic and political strife without anesthetizing audience or issue and his Attractions as a fiery yet tasteful unit that could attack reckless rockers and caress carefully constructed ballads with equal aplomb. Costello was gradually becoming accepted by the mainstream without conceding to it. And then it happened.

American pop's portrait of Costello is indelibly colored by a barroom incident in which he defamed Ray Charles as "a blind, ignorant nigger" and got his glasses knocked off his head by a has-been American pop singer. The epithets fulfilled most people's until-then muted fears about punk and continues to haunt him. This is ridiculous. Such pre-incident songs as "Less Than Zero" and "Night Rally" (and his production of a tribute to Nelson Mandela before such bromides became fashionable) underline the absurdity of labeling Costello a racist. One eyewitness to the brawl said it looked like Costello wanted to be mauled.

Costello then spent the better part of a decade scrambling for a niche, though even an indecisive Costello has merit. The 1980 *Get Happy!* was a sketchy tour through physical and moral expatriation with Stax-filtered soul as the soundtrack and *Imperial Bedroom* (1982) wove an astonishing, ambitious collage of late-Beatles pop landscapes. But then, as if that expansive album had claimed all his ideas, decline set in. Costello traded wordplay for facility and his accompaniment, once terse and unforgiving, deteriorated into dilettantism, hopping among genres with the discretion of a sailor on leave. It wasn't a complete fall; the personal venom and political acuity of early Costello occasionally slipped through the cracks of his crumbling career.

In 1984, after Costello had completed recording his most desultory album (not-so-subtly titled *Goodbye Cruel World*), he embarked on a solo tour and reclaimed his career. He shed the Attractions, whose lush backup had dulled what straightforward melodies and narratives he still conjured. He followed that tour with a short jaunt backed by the Attractions, but made clear that he had one foot out the door. "I was a fine idea at the time," he sang on one of his tight new tunes. "But now I'm a brilliant mistake." He got divorced, fell in love, and put the Attractions on hiatus. Then he recorded the album of his life.

Performers make different noises when they think—or fear—that no one is listening. *King of America* was the sound of a zombie coming back to life, or a life in fear of turning into a zombie. He identified the "kingdom of the invisible" in "Little Palaces" as the place where Prince William will reign, but that was where all these characters lived. Every line on the album was sung by narrators terrified that they will disappear, sure only that they don't matter. No one worried about the world falling apart because they were convinced it already had. The rockabilly "Glitter Gulch," on surface a light poke at American game shows that ended with the winner taking up with the hostess, railed against the crassness of any relationship. "He climbed upon his honey and he covered her with money," Costello spat. Amidst these ravages, there was a hovering love ("I'll Wear It Proudly," "Jack of All Parades") that never quite landed— but its proximity made the pain nearly bearable. The music was a lanky foundation, loose yet precise. Built around the core of Elvis Presley's last band, dubbed the Confederates (Costello finally addressing some of the ramifications of his ostentatious nickname), they squeezed inside the songs, nourishing the numbers instead of inflating them. Several years after *Almost Blue*, a tentative and rather obvious set of country-and-western standards, Costello was finally able to incorporate the personal moral profundity of top-drawer country-and-western into the public ethical demands of his most lasting work. Country ballads, Chicago blues, waltzes—everything fit in, commented on other elements, and enhanced one another.

Costello produced the record with T Bone Burnett, another hyperverbal-verging-on-cynical performer looking for a way to unclutter his mind and his music, and the combination resulted in as honest and direct an LP as Costello will likely ever record. They knew that embellishment would have been superfluous. The tunes on *King of America* justified themselves without any of the insular alterations that a studio-weary Costello later employed to deflate some of his finest early-nineties compositions. The distances—between performer and audience, between song and arrangement, between performer and song, between born name Declan MacManus and jokey stage monicker Elvis Costello—that have always fascinated Costello, even on many of his stronger outings, are totally absent on *King of America*, replaced instead by a singer and guitarist obsessed with paring away, telling the truth. Costello still loved words too much not to tinker with them; hence, lines such as "Like a chainsaw running through a dictionary," from "Our Little Angel," an ominous country ballad, built around James Burton's pointed, graceful guitar nudges, which is recommended to Merle Haggard. The difference was that this time Costello wasn't hiding behind words.

To complete his public rehabilitation, Costello cast off on a wacko tour featuring him in a variety of configurations, some profound, most amusing. For the final encore of the tour's final show, Costello chose "Poor Napoleon," a slight, funny song about impotence from *Blood and Chocolate*, the rush-recorded-but-still-worthy follow-up to *King of America*. As the tale reached its conclusion, the instruments (he was again touring with the Attractions, for what turned out to be the last time) stopped emitting notes and started shooting out distortion, until the noise turned painful. The feedback still filled the theater after the band left the stage for good and the house lights went up. Costello had brought both his band and his audience back to where they had all started, with nothing resolved.

Number Twenty-Nine

Smokey Robinson
Where There's Smoke . . .
Tamla, 1979

As the leader of the Miracles, Robinson was a lyricist on a par with Chuck Berry and a melodist more taut than Buddy Holly. His solo years, comparatively underacknowledged, were not as consistent but still had towering peaks, as evidenced by records like *Where There's Smoke . . .* The sweetest voice in pop-music history kicks off this latter-day soul landmark with the couplet: "It's a good night for staying at home/It's a good night for doing the town." This neatly encapsulates the record's musical and lyrical concerns: Stay in, stay out, but stay together. *Where There's Smoke . . .* is a make-out record, all right, but one geared for couples experienced and comfortable enough to own the homes in which they're making out.

Robinson's falsetto doesn't arch as high here as it did on his sixties Miracles rhapsodies, but in its place at the very top of his range is knowledge that has more to do with newcomers like Prince than Marvin Gaye circa *Let's Get It On,* this record's clear precursor, although, typically, Robinson drops in mildly suggestive wordplay where the Purple One might (okay, *would*) talk explicitly. Robinson splits the LP into "Smoke" and "Fire" sides, and after a side of sweet craft, the three-song second side does indeed burn. Robinson's frankly disco reworking of the Temptations hit "Get Ready" (which Smokey wrote) doesn't cut the original, but it does bring the tune into the post-*Saturday Night Fever* world without succumbing completely to the Zeitgeist.

He goes out on "Cruisin'," a ballad in his old style, but more direct. Robinson the Tamla/Motown executive may have manipulated the images connoted by the song's title to appeal to heterosexual and homosexual audiences with equal ease, but it is Robinson the romantic singer who rules here. His exhortations to a mystery ride in his car aren't only insouciant—they're a promise of travel to a better place.

Number Thirty

Jason and the Scorchers
Fervor
EMI America, 1984

In late 1983, Jason Ringenberg, lead singer of Jason and the Scorchers, balanced himself on a rickety stool in the basement of a now-boarded Philadelphia dive and wished aloud what he wanted his band to sound like. "Like a religious service," he said wistfully, "only a lot dirtier."

This is not an attitude that brings major labels running, and Jason and the Scorchers were the great lost band of the eighties, starting great and getting even better with each record, though fewer and fewer people heard them each time around. In the eighties, the music industry was simply not geared to handle an original group like Jason and the Scorchers, a ferocious hard-rock band with a strong grounding in country-and-western. Nowadays the Kentucky Headhunters, a group with similar sources, is among the most-loved bands in Nashville. If any traditional rock-and-roll band in the eighties was ahead of its time, it was Jason and the Scorchers.

The Scorcher's debut EP, 1982's *Reckless Country Soul* (hmmm, maybe I'll write a book about the best EPs of all time; naah), is the sound of Joe Strummer hurling a wrecking ball through the Grand Ol' Opry. Its standout, "Shot Down Again," starts with Ringenberg screaming, "Look out London—here come the Scorchers!" Pop-music historians of the twenty-first century will recognize this as important early evidence of the anti-eighties-hair-bands-from-England backlash.

Fervor, recorded the following year, elaborates the band's strengths. Drawing from both their country-and-western and rock-and-roll sources, the Scorchers burn a country-rock path such poseurs as the Eagles would never have found even if their dealers had given them detailed directions. Drummer Perry Baggs and bass player Jeff Johnson give Ringenberg's edgy songs a solid foundation while Warner Hodges slides from delicate lap-steel to dirty guitar-hero styles without allowing either to sound like an afterthought. The record, full of, well, scorching originals and a knock-out version of Bob Dylan's "Absolutely Sweet Marie," had the immediacy of the group's live show. Although Hodges wasn't standing at the edge of a stage sucking a cigarette and Ringenberg wasn't dancing like Ed Norton on methamphetamines, *Fervor* came across just as hard as the group did live. If there's any eighties band that has earned fan nostalgia, it's these guys.

Number Thirty-One

Robert Cray
Strong Persuader
Mercury/Hightone, 1986

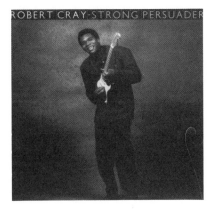

Those who claim that all blues songs nowadays sound the same—worn out—miss the point. Drawing from a thoroughly familiar storehouse doesn't have to be a liability if a performer remembers he's molding a common language and dancing on common ground. Unlike rock and roll or jazz, the most lasting blues compositions can explicitly acknowledge their genre limits. Blues does expand, mostly in fits and starts that have much to do with the mastering of recording-technology advances, but more and more the form encourages mastery, not innovation. Anyway, there are too few performers compulsive enough to explore the untapped nuances that do remain. The deterioration of blues into proficient revivalism stems more from a sparsity of iconoclasts than from terminal deficiencies in the form.

Guitarist, singer, and songwriter Robert Cray is a young bluesman only by latter-day standards (he was thirty-two when he recorded *Strong Persuader*). More than any other performer of his generation, Cray shows the determination and the flair to break out of the blues slow lane and start directing traffic. His hybrid of choice, southern-soul blues, is partly derived from Little Milton. *Strong Persuader*, Cray's fourth album, is his first for a major label, and it backs up half a decade of word-of-mouth ballyhoo. Cray hasn't gone in for any of the shake-ups that often plague established independent performers who finally get signed; he's retained his production team and all but one member of his original band.

The first side of the strident *Strong Persuader* is superb, the decade's finest sustained new blues side by a mile. Cray kicks off with the anxious variant of the "Secret Agent Man" riff that fuels "Smoking Gun" and proceeds through a pair of deliberations about infidelity from the possible victim's side ("I Guess I Showed Her") and the perpetrator's (he is the strong persuader in "Right Next Door"). The side climaxes with keyboard player Peter Boe's ominous prelude to domestic violence, "Still Around." On these tracks, Cray and band pay more sly reverence to blues feeling than blues form. Cray's finest numbers vault over genre limitations; his voice coasts over the band as do his brief, slangy guitar outbursts. This is deservedly one of the best-selling blues records of all time.

Number Thirty-Two

The Moonglows
Look! It's the Moonglows
Chess, 1956

Chicago's Chess Records is best-known for its fire-breathing urban blues from the likes of Muddy Waters, Howlin' Wolf, and Sonny Boy Williamson, and pioneering rock and roll from Chuck Berry and Bo Diddley. This reflects history, but like most great labels Chess did more than conventional wisdom suggests. Some of Chess's biggest hits, by the Moonglows, were the sweetest pop music imaginable (or, at least, the sweetest pop that didn't taste like saccharine). The Moonglows' recordings were too well-ornamented for doo-wop, and too soulful to be mistaken for straight pop. Indeed, at least two of these eleven songs are among the smartest romantic songs ever recorded, as sentimental as any Elvis Presley ballad of the time, but always satisfying. Again, there is no cloying aftertaste.

Under the direction of Harvey Fuqua, later a Marvin Gaye crony and sanitizer, fellow singers Bobby Lester and Alexander Graves, and supple guitarist Bill Johnson, the Moonglows force soft string sections to bow to them; you'll find no sob-inducing moves in these songs except for the spontaneous ones from the vocalists that no producer, however cynical, could have anticipated. The Moonglows put more terror into "Blue Velvet" than even David Lynch ever imagined, drawing and quartering each syllable so that every word breathes dread and peaceless resignation. This is beautiful music only on a surface level; the Moonglows massage you and sucker-punch you at the same time.

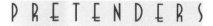

Number Thirty-Three

Pretenders
Pretenders
Sire, 1980

The Pretenders are among the most unprecedented bands in rock and roll. Led by Chrissie Hynde, a singer and songwriter from Ohio with a killer instinct like no one this side of Johnny Rotten, they exploded onto the scene and immediately altered the nomenclature on how to present and receive female performers in the context of rock and roll. Some critics have written that Hynde's greatest achievement on *Pretenders* was that she made sex distinctions irrelevant, but that's an egalitarian fantasy that takes into account neither nature (don't worry, I won't bring up Camille Paglia) nor the romantic side of Hynde's work.

Pretenders was a breakthrough because Hynde's punk-charged hard rock was even more powerful than that of the boys. Over the very end of the fade in the reggae "Lovers of Today," sung so quietly that you have to crank up your stereo to make it out at all, she intones, "I'll never feel like a man in a man's world." Anyone who thinks she wasn't in competition doesn't understand Hynde.

Confrontations run all through this nearly hour-long LP. In "Precious," Hynde wonders whether she's pregnant and concludes, "Not me baby/I'm too precious/Fuck off." "Up the Neck," which does not refer only to a guitar, turns on the line "Lust turns to anger/A kiss to a slug." Even one of the record's sweetest songs, "Kid," powered by James Honeymoon-Scott's army of overdubbed guitar jangles, anticipates brutality. Yet there's rapprochement to go along with all this, and that's where Honeymoon-Scott, bassist Pete Farndon, and drummer Martin Chambers prove their versatility; on the covetous "Brass in Pocket" and the loving reworking of the Kinks' obscure "Stop Your Sobbing," the band slides into a midtempo groove that suggested that this band could last forever.

They didn't. Within three years of the release of *Pretenders*, the group released a disappointing follow-up, and Honeymoon-Scott and Farndon died of drug overdoses. And although she has made some fine records since then (particularly *Learning to Crawl*), Hynde has never been the same. It didn't matter; she had already changed the rules for good.

Number Thirty-Four

Jackie Wilson
The Jackie Wilson Story
Epic, 1983

Because he sang a lot of crap, Jackie Wilson didn't get the credit he deserved as one of the greatest of all rhythm-and-blues vocalists. Performance in pop music is more important than composition (would you rather hear Otis Redding sing a bad song or Mariah—rhymes with pariah—Carey sing a good one?), but throughout Wilson's career the songs he put across were often so absurdly bad it was hard to get at the astonishingly imaginative pipes behind them. Until this set, that is.

The Jackie Wilson Story features twenty-four cuts that reveal how slick rhythm and blues can get without devolving into lowest-common-denominator pop. Compilers Joe McEwen and Gregg Geller have put together a compilation that completely recontextualizes Wilson's work. Instead of a typical Wilson album, with one or two non-hack compositions out of the whole bunch, McEwen and Geller reverse the usual percentage.

Some of Wilson's non-Borscht Belt ballads, like "To Be Loved" (one of several early hits), are persuasive, though more weighed down than the slow-down numbers he used to sing with the Dominoes (the vocal group with Billy Ward and Clyde McPhatter, not the band that recorded "Layla"). The uptempo cuts, moving faster so some of the clutter fell off, were more agreeable vehicles. In performance with the Dominoes, Wilson gave an exceptional Elvis Presley impression, and his first single as a solo act, "Reet Petite," was a hiccupping rocker that owed much to Elvis's version of "Don't Be Cruel." Wilson excelled on other early uptempo numbers like "Lonely Teardrops" and "Baby Workout," but his greatest hit, "(Your Love Keeps Lifting Me) Higher and Higher," didn't come until almost a decade later, after years of chicken soup.

"(Your Love Keeps Lifting Me) Higher and Higher" might be the happiest song in all pop music, from the swooping bass line that starts the number to Wilson's falsetto cries in the chorus to the greatest use of strings in a pop song (you can find the only competition for this title in the coda to the Rolling Stones' "Sway"). Years after all but his most die-hard fans assumed he was washed up, Wilson was given a number worthy of his talent and he scorched. This collection may be rendered redundant by Rhino's upcoming box set, but it is unlikely that Wilson will ever be better served in a single-disc collection.

Number Thirty-Five

Roy Orbison
*For the Lonely: A Roy Orbison
Anthology, 1956–1965*
Rhino, 1987

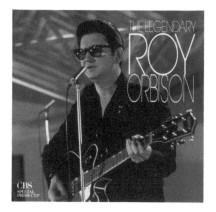

Be grateful you didn't suffer through the adolescence of any of the protagonists in Roy Orbison's songs. In sixties hits on Monument like "I'm Hurtin'," "Only the Lonely," "Crying," "Running Scared," "In Dreams," and a dozen more, paranoia, self-pity, and pathological loneliness bedevil profoundly unsettled teenagers, albeit ones who can articulate their terrors with operatic range and grace. In all these songs, Orbison draws us in and makes us care about these characters, partly because we're relieved that we're not any of them.

Orbison's catalog was a mess in the years before his triumphant comeback. About all one could find with any regularity were scattered Sun reissues (often badly padded) and a skimpy Monument best-of. Thanks in part to the acrid impact "In Dreams" had in David Lynch's *Blue Velvet*, Orbison rebounded, as did his older recordings. *For the Lonely: A Roy Orbison Anthology, 1956–1965* is a double-LP, 24-track anthology of original recordings for both Sun and Monument, bolstered by unusually clear and unobtrusive remixing and remastering. (Consumer warning: the CD version of this set sacrifices six songs to keep royalty costs down. For digital-audio fans, the best choice is *The Legendary Roy Orbison*, a four-CD box from CBS that has problems but is very thorough.)

By placing four of Orbison's raucous 1956–1957 Sun tracks beside his more mannered Monument highlights, this set makes his move to the Nashville label sound like an extension of his Sun sound, not a direct contradiction. Sure, the instrumentation was denser, strings and background choruses cushioning vocal angst, but all of Orbison's material, whether produced by Sam Phillips at Sun or Fred Foster at Monument, sounded compressed by design. "Mean Woman Blues" (a Number Five smash in

1963) is a turbulent, bluesabilly Jerry Lee Lewis *hommage*, though it was recorded for Monument. When Orbison offered up an unexpected dark growl, in "Oh, Pretty Woman," his biggest hit, the leering he let loose was a sound that he had picked up under Phillips's tutelage, not Foster's.

Still, it was Orbison's Monument work that got him voted into the Rock-and-Roll Hall of Fame. *For the Lonely* offers a broad selection of the stuff, from his characteristic teen melodramas to the occasional aggressive stomper like "Workin' for the Man." But in every one of these Monument sides, Orbison sounds tortured, be it by his job, his circumstances, his memory, his soon-to-be-ex-girlfriend, or himself. We hear the sweeping arrangements in ballads like "Blue Bayou" and "It's Over" as truly serene. In wanders Orbison's voice and we hear ravagement. No one articulated teen terror with more adult wisdom than Orbison; no one else could make such pain feel like a kiss.

Number Thirty-Six

Ted Hawkins
On the Boardwalk
American Activities, 1986

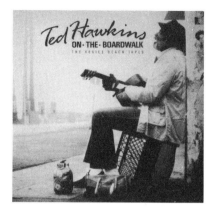

The amateur roots of the most heartfelt pop music is inarguable. Great performers who have reached megaplatinum status can come up with songs and performances that cut to the core (Bruce Springsteen does it all the time, and John Lennon pulled it off more often than not). But rock and roll is full of performers whose debut album so far exceeds anything else they have ever done you'd wish they'd go flying with Ritchie Valens. It's no romantic cliché to suggest that great art might be more likely to emerge out of hunger. The Springsteens and Lennons of the world can transfer physical hunger to emotional hunger, but the former is much more prevalent. The greatest of all work often comes from performers who are singing for their supper.

I mean this literally, and there's no better evidence for this than *On the Boardwalk*, a pair of LPs by Ted Hawkins. Hawkins is a phenomenal singer, agile in all styles, favoring the intersection between soul and blues. His two albums for Rounder, *Watch Your Step* and *Happy Hour*, recorded by Robert Cray's producer Bruce Bromberg before and after Hawkins did time in prison, are astonishingly direct, precise, impassioned. His writing is amazing—in "Bad Dog" he discovers that his lover is having an affair because her ill-tempered dog treats a stranger with surprising tenderness—and his performances veer on the edge of heartbreak. Hawkins frequently sounds like he's singing at the edge of his range and this tension lends the songs more impact.

On the Boardwalk covers the repertoire Hawkins plays on the boardwalk in Venice Beach, California. Playing for quarters and dollars is how he made his living at one point, accompanied only by an acoustic guitar. Nearly all the twenty-eight songs on *On the Boardwalk* are other people's hits, ranging from Sam Cooke's "Good Times" (Cooke is Hawkins's pre-eminent vocal influence) to songs associated with Johnny Horton, Bob Dylan, Webb Pierce, Otis Redding, Hank Williams, Paul Simon, and many more. The term "stripped-down" only begins to describe these performances, put across with the urgency of someone staring at people's hands to see if they will reach into their pockets. And if they do, so what? He knows he'll be back tomorrow, and his dreams can earn a brief life only in his repertoire.

Number Thirty-Seven

Stevie Wonder
Innervisions
Tamla, 1973

Stevie Wonder's first album was titled *Little Stevie Wonder, the 12 Year Old Genius,* and although Motown probably awarded Wonder the appellation for superficial reasons (like the existing genius of soul, Ray Charles, Wonder was blind), he had earned such attention immediately upon his arrival. His wonder years, catalogued on a wondrous triple-album called *Looking Back,* are full of amazingly diverse hits, from the thrilling scatting of "Fingertips Pt. 2" to the puppy love of "My Cherie Amour," then back again to the riotous "Uptight," his finest Motown-formula-conforming single.

Still a teenager, Wonder put across a convincing, original version of Bob Dylan's "Blowin' in the Wind"; it was clear early on in a career that will probably go on into the next century that his interest ranged far beyond what was normally acceptable at Motown. Yet Wonder's maturation into adulthood gave him the opportunity to write and record what he wanted. This happened while other great Motown performers, like Marvin Gaye and the Temptations, were also feeling their oats, and for a brief time the label seemed like a place where freedom had no limits. Wonder's hits continued, no matter what he chose to cut.

Of his breakthrough early-seventies albums, when, along with Sly Stone, Wonder discovered that he was stretching the limits of what African-American pop could include, the most visionary of them was undoubtedly *Innervisions.* Wonder's clear voice was always a pleasing presence, though in particular situations, like the devastating final verse of "Living for the City," he could reveal his rage by roughening his delivery. *Innervisions* is an interconnected suite of songs—many of them segue right into each other—but it's not of the navel-gazing variety

76

implied in the typically hazy album title. "Living for the City," "Higher Ground," and "He's Misstra Know-It-All" are among Wonder's most trenchant world-aware tunes, and "Too High" examines insularity unsparingly. Wonder plays nearly every instrument on his record, and this do-it-yourself confidence inspired many who were listening, particularly a Minneapolis kid named Prince Rogers Nelson.

It's inarguable that Wonder has softened in recent years. Still, he's no fossil, as I was pleased to discover at an arena show in 1986. The truest moment of the three-hours-plus performance arrived midway through "Superstition" (from *Talking Book*), when he unleashed a scathing, hideous scream, as if he'd awoken from a bad dream. Immediately, he realized he'd gone too far, stepped back, and meekly reentered the song, a bit embarrassed by the outburst. Stevie Wonder smiled. He was comfortable again.

Number Thirty-Eight

Patsy Cline
Stop, Look, and Listen
MCA, 1986

Until recently, the catalogue of this great country singer, whose velvet voice marked the height of the Nashville sound in country and western, was a mess. The double-LP collection that for long had to set the standard, *The Patsy Cline Story*, was marred by posthumous overdubs, and the soundtrack to 1985's overrated film *Sweet Dreams* (yeah, right; like Jessica Lange had a clue) was even worse. I am a guarded fan of Cline's producer Owen Bradley, especially guarded since he grafted a saxophone onto "Blue Moon of Kentucky" for the movie, and in doing so destroyed any cultural context. Watch out.

Anyway, the reissue campaign that MCA inaugurated in the wake of the success (box-office success, anyway) of *Sweet Dreams* sent matters back in the right direction. Cline made her name with the country ballads in the late fifties and early sixties that emerged as a response to renegade rockabilly, but her arching voice was just as compatible with other country stylings. That's where *Stop, Look, and Listen*, compiled by Jay Orr, then of the Country Music Foundation, fits in.

In late 1955, before Bradley made ballads the rule for his charge, he experimented with some more uptempo tunes, including some borderline rockabilly romps. None of Cline's rawer material drew much of an audience, but her heated runs through these twelve tracks point to a more raucous future than "Crazy" or "Sweet Dreams." There are ballads here, most notably the lush "Shoes," but the most representative and most spirited tune is the title number. Like a country-and-western La Vern Baker (a title to which Wanda Jackson also had pretensions), Cline bruises, cruises, and testifies without manners or mannerisms, just the joy of release. This is a Cline most fans never knew existed, and one Bradley should have let out of the cage more often. After she moved up to Decca, Cline hinted at her power in performances like "Walking After Midnight," but at 4-Star she was more comfortable shouting her brave affirmations of freedom. Some claim that the mannered Nashville Sound of the late fifties and sixties was geared to Cline's voice, and *Stop, Look, and Listen* showcases the strength and tenacity with which she transformed Nashville.

Although *Stop, Look, and Listen* is the best single Cline CD available, those'in search of more are directed to *The Patsy Cline Collection*, a four-CD set including *Honky Tonk Merry Go Ground* that takes in all her Decca recordings, the best of her 4-Star cuts, rarities worth the trouble, and brilliant sound.

Number Thirty-Nine

Burning Spear
Garvey's Ghost
Mango, 1976

Burning Spear's *Marcus Garvey* was stirring and heady, a broadside for what was then a little-known way (in this country, anyway) of hearing reggae. The cover photo of the trio leaning at odd angles in front of wood planks seems shot beside a slave ship, and singer Winston Rodney turns righteous drama into joyous keening. Joe Strummer's ideas about expansive rhythms started here.

Indeed, the album's instrumental counterpart, *Garvey's Ghost*, solidified the idea of dub as a rhythm zone or a kind of sound playing-field that can be endlessly revisited and revised. The tracks eschew the rough-hewn top melodies of the straight version and zoom in on its low-profile countermelodies. Echoed horns dart in and out of focus; Rodney's vocals are rarely audible, deployed only to underline a mood that the instruments are already conveying, especially the pained cries on the fervid "I and I Survive"; and rhythm guitarist Valentine Chin anchors the beat as drummer Leroy Wallace dances around it. Producer L. Lindo (a.k.a. Jack Ruby, not the Dallas club owner) places Robbie Shakespeare's and Aston "Family Man" Barret's sturdy bass figures as far up front as he can stick them without letting them fall out of the speakers.

At its best, dub shines light on aspects of songs that the original version sometimes gave short shrift. *Garvey's Ghost*, along with records from Big Youth, King Tubby, the great Lee Perry, and others, helped set the style for the whole dub sweep that followed and still influences such hip-hop mixer/producers as Arthur Baker and Public Enemy's Terminator X. *Garvey's Ghost* means to make its listener feel cramped inside the slave ship along with the band. When they get to their final "Resting Place," they mean us to remain uneasy with them too. The sound you hear is the galleon sinking.

Consumer note: *Marcus Garvey* and *Garvey's Ghost* are available together on one compact disc.

Number Forty

Ry Cooder
Paradise and Lunch
Reprise, 1974

The best gospel-influenced album ever made by latter-day white rounders is a wide-open barrel through sundry genres of American music that's always fun and never stuffy. Ry Cooder is one of rock and pop's most brainy virtuosos on stringed instruments, and on *Paradise and Lunch* he mixes techniques he admires in guitar masters like Bahamian Joseph Spence with the mindful good times of early rock and roll, and he cruises.

The wry (sorry) arrangements on *Paradise and Lunch* sound like they are held together with thin string, high spirits, and Cooder's dry and tattered vocals. On tunes as ostensibly disparate as the traditional "Jesus on the Mainline" and Blind Willie McTell's admonishing "Married Man's a Fool," Cooder's sputtering bottleneck guitar locks into the rhythm section and drolly lets the tale unwind. Religious images permeate nearly every track, with strings and horns wreathed with pre-Broadway decorum.

Listen, learn, and dance. It is Cooder's catholic tastes, most evident at the end of the sides, that elevate *Paradise and Lunch* the highest. Side One finishes with a gnarled reggae reading of Bobby and Shirley Womack's "It's All Over Now," a bitterly mulled-over assignation that develops into a slinky dance. The album ends with a six-minute acoustic-guitar-and-piano duet featuring Cooder and Earl "Fatha" Hines on Arthur Blake's "Ditty Wa Ditty." The sensibly nonsensical lyrics drift in and out and finally drop away, allowing Cooder and Hines to trade smiles, solos, and loose rhythms. *Paradise and Lunch* is a low-key triumph, and an enriching roller-coaster ride of a history lesson. If school was this much fun, we'd all be musicologists.

Number Forty-One

Sam and Dave
The Best of Sam and Dave
Atlantic, 1987

These days, notions of Sam and Dave are wrapped up in nostalgia and Dan Aykroyd imitations, but during their late sixties peak the pleading pair were second at Stax only to Otis Redding. Both Sam Moore and Dave Prater started singing in church (Sam nearly joined the Soul Stirrers as Sam Cooke's replacement), and each of them was working solo when they met in Miami. Their voices were noticeably different, but not wildly disparate, much like the Righteous Brothers' Bill Medley and Bobby Hatfield. Each thrived in solo settings, yet each leaned on the other at every turn in these twenty-one recordings.

The Best of Sam and Dave is an expanded version of a decade's old greatest-hits collection, in spectacular sound. The songs here are a testament not only to the supple, agile voices of Moore and Prater and the usual sympatico backing by Stax's house band, but also to the producers at Stax. The first half is supervised by label head Jim Stewart and he hands Sam and Dave all the rope they need to thrive through the one-two-punch horns of "A Place Nobody Can Find" and other cuts that inexorably burrow toward emotional truths. Their biggest hit, "Soul Man," is still explosive today, in spite of the Blues Brothers' unintentional trivialization of the song. The number's spontaneous vocal asides (like the famous "Play it, Steve" order to guitarist Steve Cropper) and swirling horns, not to mention Cropper's rhythmic leads, make "Soul Man" perfectly self-descriptive. It's all delightful self-affirmation, with no ego in the way. All singers and musicians on the track delight in their abilities: When you hear Moore and Prater sing "Got what I got the hard way," you know the work paid off. The second half is produced by Isaac Hayes and Dave Porter, who provide the pair with now much-covered compositions like "I Thank You" and "Wrap It Up." Compared to Stewart, the method of Hayes and Porter is simultaneously rougher and more accommodating. Yet it's all part of one method, built around two magnificent, committed voices. Atlantic is currently in the process of reissuing the duo's original albums from their classic period; all are wholeheartedly recommended.

Number Forty-Two

Parliament
The Clones of Dr. Funkenstein
Casablanca, 1976

So what if George Clinton, the leader of Parliament, Funkadelic, the P-Funk All-Stars, and half a dozen lesser units, is a ripoff artist? As the Parliaments, this group started out with the 1967 rhythm-and-blues smash "(I Just Wanna) Testify," but Clinton's muse was too diffuse and ambitious to be contained by a form he considered traditional and thus confining. With the possible exception of the mammoth 1978 Funkadelic set *One Nation Under a Groove*, Clinton's greatest work was with Parliament, the purest and most visionary of his funk-minded ensembles.

Throughout the seventies, Parliament was remarkably consistent—albums like *Up for the Down Stroke, Mothership Connection,* and *Funketelchy vs. the Placebo Syndrome*—are as deep, dark, and wide-ranging as you'd suspect from the titles. The live shows of the period were completely out to lunch, full of spaceship landings and simulated sex. But the funniest, funkiest, hammiest distillation of Clinton's propulsive weirdness was the 1976 LP *The Clones of Dr. Funkenstein.* On this record, Parliament is the anti-Earth, Wind, and Fire.

"Funk is its own reward. May I frighten you?" Clinton intones at the end of the record's portentous introduction, and the fear is felt by those without open minds. The lyrics on *The Clones of Dr. Funkenstein* are the usual science-fiction doggerel—it's a witty tale of creating the perfect funky man and woman through cloning. (Remember cloning? It was a big deal around the same time as the Bermuda Triangle and Farrah Fawcett.) As usual for Clinton, the words on *The Clones of Dr. Funkenstein* are amusing excuses for him and his army to use the word "funk" in barbed and unexpected ways in the midst of all the synthesized bass lines and strutting guitar that grounded P-Funk. This mix remains influential to many; Clinton now records for a label owned by Prince, which seems logical.

Number Forty-Three

The Contours
*Do You Love Me (Now That
I Can Dance)*
Motown, 1967

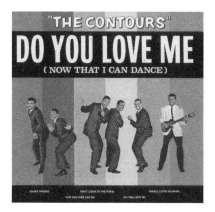

In many ways, Motown Records was about control, both corporate (Berry Gordy kept his staff on short leashes) and musical (most of its first-line performers cultivated restraint in their performances, so much so that even hand claps sounded terse). At the label, the raving Contours—singers Billy Gordon, Billy Hoggs, Joe Billingstea, Sylvester Potter, Hubert Johnson, and singer/guitarist Huey Davis—were a welcome anomaly.

Their first hit, which gives this collection its title, was penned and produced by Gordy in 1962, and it is wild. Based loosely on the Isley Brothers' "Twist and Shout," it starts slowly, just Davis's guitar and Gordon telling how he lost his woman because he couldn't twirl his pins well enough. The last line of the introduction announces that the problem has been remedied, and an early incarnation of Motown's session band crashes in, breaking leashes. The singer shows off his mastery of the mashed potato, the jerk, the twist, you name it.

Nothing else here was as big a hit for the Contours, though many must have been listening. Peter Wolf scooped "First I Look at the Purse" for the debut J. Geils Band album, and dance tunes like "Shake Sherrie" and "Can You Jerk Like Me" were popular among early-sixties club stalwarts. And then there's "You Get Ugly," which is either hilarious or deeply sexist. It's definitely weird; it's too bad Gordy (who considered the Contours "a bunch of hoodlums") didn't encourage his performers to speak out more.

Consumer warning: The CD version of this record doesn't have the original version of the title hit but a truly stupid disco remix, which eliminates the false fade of the original and virtually everything else about the original that was any good. Yucch.

Number Forty-Four

Richard and Linda Thompson
Shoot Out the Lights
Hannibal, 1982

The cult that has grown around *Shoot Out the Lights* is one built on romantic assumptions that actually undermine the greatness of Richard and Linda Thompson's crowning achievement. *Shoot Out the Lights* is a collection of eight Richard Thompson tunes (one of them a rare number cowritten with wife Linda) that explore the musical and lyrical themes that fascinated Thompson since the guitarist and singer founded the signal British folk-rock group Fairport Convention more than fifteen years earlier: romantic and moral dangers that spring from the intersection of rock and roll and various pre-rock traditional forms. *Shoot Out the Lights* is not, as many fans and critics have blurted out, an album that explicitly—or even metaphorically—documents the disintegration of the relationship between the principals.

The Thompsons's marriage ended around the time this album was recorded (for once life justified legend: Linda broke a beer bottle on Richard's head on the final night of their ill-fated tour supporting the album), which suggested to even well-intentioned listeners that they had license to read all sorts of personal messages throughout *Shoot Out the Lights*. "Don't Renege on Our Love" was said to be about a last-ditch attempt to keep their relationship going, "Walking on Wire" deliberated on the inevitable failure of such an attempt, and so on. Critics (and, to a lesser degree, fans) think they're being sensitive when they tighten these straitjackets about the songs, but these listeners are really betraying that they have less respect than they claim for the imagination of Thompson as a writer. Because they have trouble looking outside themselves when trying to think or write creatively (a common rock-critic malady), they assume that their heroes can't jump out either. There is no doubt that the principals' personal tension when *Shoot Out the Lights* was recorded is part of why these performances are so great, but for once let's examine these songs as works of art rather than marriage-therapy transcripts.

Except for the silly, I-gotta-ramble-baby "A Man in Need," every song on *Shoot Out the Lights* features Richard's guitar and Richard and Linda's voices picking at sores, probing beneath surfaces, hunting for truths, praying that those truths won't disappoint. The dead woman in "Did She Jump or Was She Pushed?," the boy hunting for unnamed danger in "The Wall of Death," the killer in the title track (one of the many songs on the album which Richard has subsequently surpassed in performing live)— all these characters are looking for some sort of escape, some sort of answer. None find any, although the act of searching for cues, spilling into Thompson's modal, circular guitar outbursts, provided its own sustenance. All this makes *Shoot Out the Lights* one of the most yearning records in all rock and roll.

Cult worship aside, this record isn't perfect. Dave Mattacks's drums sometimes sound muffled compared to what he could do with them live (big exception: the booming floor-tom crack that climaxes "Shoot Out the Lights"), and the extra track on the CD, "Living in Luxury," is lightweight. But these are trifles for those of us who have reveled in the music of Richard Thompson, the *Pilgrim's Progress* extended guitar solos in "Calvary Cross" and "For Shame of Doing Wrong," the remarkably vivid pessimism of "End of the Rainbow" and "Withered and Died."

For further investigation, nearly every one of Richard Thompson's post-Fairport Convention albums, both with and without Linda, are riveting (the best might be the 1988 Capitol album *Amnesia* but one could just as easily make a strong case for *I Want To See the Bright Lights Tonight, Pour Down Like Silver,* or the recent *Rumor and Sigh*), and Richard Thompson has developed into one of the most consistent live performers of the late 1980s. Almost every night, he'll play at least one selection of *Shoot Out the Lights*, and a decade after their release, the hunger of those songs still astounds.

Number Forty-Five

Hank Williams Jr.
Hank Williams Jr. and Friends
MGM, 1975

If you had been trapped as a safe-appendage to your father for your whole life, you'd rebel too. By the time he turned twenty-six, Hank Williams Jr. had personified the expected myth: married and divorced twice, both parents dead, most of his face scraped off during a five-hundred-foot tumble down a mountain. Before the accident he had released numerous albums with numerous tracks that approximated his father's deathly quaver on—surprise!—Dad's tunes. So on *Hank Williams Jr. and Friends*, the first album on which Junior cupped his ear to hear anything outside the slick Nashville Zeitgeist (duller than it is now, if you can imagine that) and prodded by the discontent stirring in Texas and elsewhere, Williams decided he was a hale member of the rock-and-roll generation, not an automated torch-bearer for his father.

All but three songs on *Hank Williams Jr. and Friends* are by the artist. Two of the three outside numbers are Marshall Tucker Band numbers, written by guitarist Toy Caldwell, whose slide playing on his trembling "Can't You See" delicately paraphrases the singer's anguish. Hank Jr.'s compositions concentrate on his idea of survival. After the honky-tonk stagger (or is that swagger?) "Stoned at the Jukebox," the album ends with the autobiographical "Living Proof." A wobbly Hank Jr. bumps into an old drunk who damns him, screaming that he'll never live up to his father, no matter how hard he tries. For the length of the song, the insult and the false comparison (Dmitri Nabokov has written a novel and it's pretty good, but nobody had a right to expect it to be *Pale Fire*) knock Hank Jr. sober, at least for the length of the song. Both Hank Jr.'s career and his life go on, both full of missteps, but at least after this most of his missteps are his own, not someone else's. Since then, Bocephus (Junior's childhood nickname, to which he still answers, which should tell you something) has allowed himself to be portrayed as a buffoon. Clearly, his self-awareness quickly dissipated. So what? His transformation left this the finest country-rock fusion of the decade from the country side, with the possible exception of Joe Ely's *Honky Tonk Masquerade*.

Number Forty-Six

Bob Marley and the Wailers
Catch a Fire
Island, 1973

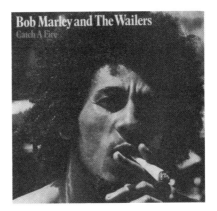

Although in the last of his too-few years Bob Marley deteriorated into a mere popularizer of reggae music, he started out as a true innovator. Under the wing of Jamaican pop icon Joe Higgs, the teenaged Marley formed the Wailers with Peter Tosh and Neville "Bunny" Livingston and two other members, and came up with a vocal-group sound that suggested a tenser brand of doo-wop. These early years are well-documented on *The Birth of a Legend (1963–66)* (Epic) and *One Love* (Heartbeat), both of which are highly recommended. In 1969 the Wailers—the Marley, Tosh, Livingston vocal trio plus the rhythm section of Aston "Family Man" Barrett and drummer Carlton "Carlie" Barrett—hooked up with producer Lee Perry. The last two were crucial members of Perry's studio band, the Upsetters, and they made slashing reggae records (listen to *Soul Revolution I and II* on Trojan) that were very popular in Jamaica but couldn't break out of the island. Marley started writing for American pop singer Johnny Nash, and the group seemed doomed to being well-known in an extremely small market.

Chris Blackwell, owner of Island Records, changed all that. Blackwell's commercial acumen, inarguable as always, led him to sign the group and work to break them out internationally. Knowing that the pop audience bought records by people, not some amorphous overseas pop movement, he changed the name of the group to Bob Marley and the Wailers, setting the stage for the departure of Tosh and Livingston in 1974. Marley's remarkably coherent visions, unlikely when Rastafarian concerns predominate, and his charismatic personality (captured on the recent Island anthology *Talkin' Blues*) went a long way toward making these new rhythms palatable Stateside.

Catch a Fire was the group's first Island record, their first conceived as a full-length LP, and it remains their finest. Loping guitars carry the group (this was one of the first lasting reggae albums with a top-heavy mix), and the attitude and occasional fury here owe more to traditional rock-and-roll groups like the Rolling Stones than reggae vocal groups; it's no accident that Peter Tosh eventually wound up signed to the Stones' label. Everything on the record moves hearts and feet. Among its many instant reggae standards, the ones that remain most open-ended and inviting are the chunky "Stir It Up" and the experimental "Midnight Ravers," the latter of which approximates a trenchtown version of Booker T. and the MG's. Marley's not the only lead singer; this is very much a group, as proved again in the nearly equal follow-up, *Burnin'*, which featured more well-known songs like "Get Up, Stand Up," and "I Shot the Sheriff."

On his own, the decisive Marley record is the 1975 recorded-in-London *Live* set, though never were Marley, Tosh, and Livingston more impressive than when they worked together.

Number Forty-Seven

Rank and File
Sundown
Slash, 1982

Back when roots-rock seemed a viable possibility, Austin-outsiders-turned-LA-punks-turned-country-rockers were among the vanguards of many movements. The hybrid of Rank and File wasn't as history-minded as that of contemporaries Jason and the Scorchers, but this group's more intellectual and considered bridging of American-music cultures was nearly as intoxicating. On *Sundown*, their debut album, brothers Tony and Chip Kinman were revealed to own two of the most distinctive and complementary voices of the new decade. Tony's studied baritone suggested a punk Johnny Cash, whereas Chip's quavery Lefty Frizzell tenor hovered over the songs he sang, occasionally swooping down to make some deadpan point.

The Kinmans were veterans of the Dils—an important, unknown band that played punk before its members had heard the Ramones, the Sex Pistols, or the Clash. And the nihilism of Los Angeles-style punk influenced Rank and File's lyrics as much as Merle Haggard encouraged some of their attitudes. "Things she does make me glad I'm not in love." "Today was gonna be my lucky day." "I don't go out much anymore." The words of every one of *Sundown*'s nine songs posit Rank and File as outsiders both socially and musically. In the sprightly "I Went Walking," a bewildered Chip walks through New York's St. Mark's Place, bravely announces that he'll never fall prey to such pretension as he's seen there, and prepares to move on. Then he remembers. Without any antecedent (in the song, that is; this device goes back to Ernest Tubb), he recalls a woman who left him and he wanders away from the song. It's even darker

93

on "The Conductor Wore Black," the story of a train being passed in the other direction by Woody Guthrie's bound-for-glory locomotive.

There's a sadness in every one of *Sundown*'s narrators, be they illegal aliens, union workers, or aghast lovers. Razor-thin country two-step rhythms propel most of these songs, only to end up cutting the singers. *Sundown* hurts; its performances imply that the sun may never rise again.

Number Forty-Eight

Various Performers
The Nonesuch Explorer: Music from Distant Corners of the World
Nonesuch, 1971

Last time out, Owen and I wrote "Rock and roll is but one small part of the music being made on this planet. Rockers who think they're changing the world are in fact reaching only a small part of it." The flip side to this is that open-minded performers can pick up strong ideas outside the typical U.S. and U.K. parameters. (Many of these places are former U.S. or U.K. colonies, but that's another book.) That's the idea of *The Nonesuch Explorer: Music from Distant Corners of the World*, a sampler from Nonesuch's important Explorer series. No doubt this series got in the hands of some carpetbaggers (are you listening, Paul Simon?), but its overall impact has been extremely positive. In general, music from all around the world has more of a presence in U.S. record stores—the collection *The Indestructible Beat of Soweto* (Shanachie) says more about South Africa than a week of news reports—but this is where to start.

I'm not sure that Trinidad or Greece belong among the "distant corners of the world," but that's a minor quibble. This is a groundbreaking (er, *literally* groundbreaking on one of the African work songs) collection. Put out by the premier international custom label long before such interests were trendy among the rock-and-roll congnoscenti, this inexpensive double-LP set is a glorious introduction to music that, in more diluted form, has been at the forefront of most recent cerebral-rock trends.

Each of the four sides concentrates on a different area of the world; untutored ears should probably start with the seven short tracks on the third side, which cover Africa and the Americas. It journeys from the sweet Colombian lullaby "Me voy a Belèn" to the ominous Paraguayan folk chant "El Chupino," along the way taking in percussive Rhodesian snaps and a Peruvian panpipe ensemble that delivers a particularly weightless, timeless performance. Nonesuch's African LPs are especially worth owning, if only to discover that Brian Eno and David Byrne swiped most of their collaborative-period ideas off of them.

For rock-and-roll fans, *The Nonesuch Explorer* is humbling, an expansive reminder that rock doesn't rule the planet and that much music that owes nothing to Western pop is as passionate and full of tradition as any of our revered forms. Indeed, many selections from this academic but never-stuffy compilation strike a blow against categorization in music.

Number Forty-Nine

Gary U.S. Bonds
On the Line
EMI America, 1982

Gary "U.S. Bonds" Anderson is best known for his wonderful, boister-ous party records for Legrand in the early sixties that sounded like they were recorded in airplane hangars. The saxophone-driven hits—"New Orleans," "Quarter to Three," "School Is Out," and the inevitable fol-low-up "School Is In"—were among the loudest rock-and-roll records ever made, no small achievement. Bonds's voice was a cut above that of most frat-party singers, but along with producer Frank Guida he had clearly lucked onto a formula that would keep him a strong draw in oldies shows as long as concert promoter Richard Nader was still alive. And, it seemed, that was that.

Bruce Springsteen was a fan of Bonds's, which makes sense considering the Jersey Devil's commitment to junk rock as well as the more lofty stuff. In 1981 Springsteen rescued Bonds from the nostalgia circuit. Along with E Street Band guitarist Steve Van Zandt producing, they recorded *Dedi-cation*, a strong comeback record with the sonic whirl of Springsteen's contemporaneous *The River* that greatly expanded notions of what Bonds could handle vocally. The set included songs by Jackson Browne and Bob Dylan and a custom-written tune by Van Zandt, "Daddy's Come Home," that seemed to tell the whole story of how soul music and the lives it touched had aged and changed. The record was a big hit. Its follow-up, *On the Line,* was a relative dud (no Top Twenty singles), but it was a far more substantial collection.

If *Dedication* was all about the thrill of (re)discovery, *On the Line* was about sustaining what has been found. In songs like the updated Stax rocker "Hold On (To What You Got)" and the Coasters homage "Out of Work," Bonds stretched, no longer merely delighted that he could play with the big boys, but now determined to outrun them. His party instincts enlivened his duet with a charmingly atonal Van Zandt, "Angelyne," a rewrite of Chuck Berry's "You Never Can Tell," but his heart was in the ballads, particularly "Love's on the Line," one of Springsteen's most classically constructed ballads. It's a tale of a relationship that once held everything but now seems empty. It was abstract enough that it could have referred to a relationship, a career, or both, and Bonds sang it both ways. He could handle it.

Number Fifty

Wilbert Harrison
Let's Work Together
Sue, 1969

Soul man Wilbert Harrison has never gotten his due, either for his eccentricity (Harrison was one of the few R&B-oriented one-man bands) or his classicism (this album's pained "Stand By Me" towers over even Ben E. King's dignified, dramatic treatment).

Harrison's only major smash, 1959's "Kansas City" (here in rere-corded form), is more closely identified with Little Richard and the Beatles than with the Harrison, who topped the *Billboard* pop chart with it. Even worse, this comeback sprint ran out of commercial gas rather quickly; the title tune was a minor hit, but the LP peaked at Number One Hundred and Ninety and disappeared—and that may just have been the work of a fan at *Billboard.*

The bluesy single "Let's Work Together" summed up the evils of turn-of-the-decade strife and called for camaraderie so tersely and artlessly that only cynics would refuse to stand up with the singer. Harrison's voice is prettier than, say, Wilson Pickett's, but the clarity in his natural voice makes it even more sensational when he gets rough, as he does in his "Soul Rattler." Harrison's version of the Stagger Lee myth is rather tame, but his "What Am I Living For" (Chuck Willis's big posthumous hit) is so mournful that it begs the answer "Nothing." Harrison's stamp is still around—every bar band vamps through his valiant version of "Kansas City," and everyone from Bryan Ferry to Tom Petty to Dwight Yoakam has sung "Let's Work Together"—but this record is the model of the obscure soul-cult favorite.

Number Fifty-One

The Firesign Theater
Everything You Know Is Wrong
Columbia, 1974

Or, what to do when aliens appear at your door looking for playmates.

On this, arguably the comedy group's most initially coherent and least overtly Joycean work, mankind confronts semi-intelligent life from elsewhere and, well, freaks out. *Everything You Know Is Wrong* is another shining example of how rock attitude need not be confined to rock music.

The star here is "Dr." Harry Cox, an impeccably drawn but poorly dressed caricature of Eric von Daniken (he of *Chariots of the Gods* and other ancient-astronauts hysterics). Through his low-wattage radio show, Cox shares with his Seekers tales of dogs from outer space and argues that Benjamin Franklin was a heavy dope user. (Well, he did wear the same type of sunglasses as the Byrds' Roger McGuinn.) Other memorable characters liberally dispersed throughout the album's forty-two minutes include nudist-trailer-camp director Art Wholeflaffer, "mindboggler" Nino Savatte (whose parapsychological claims make Uri Geller seem subtle and dignified), and expatriate Nazis (or are they aliens as well?) who hang out in South America and eat moss. And then there's famed daredevil motorcyclist Reebus Cannebus (any similarity to dopey racist Evel Knievel is purely intentional), who puts out the Sun in the Center of the Earth and leads mankind to a higher form of breakfast. Aliens, apparently, have infiltrated our scrambled eggs.

As with most Firesign LPs, *Everything You Know Is Wrong* is as dense as Ed Norton; as with great rock-and-roll records, only carefully repeated listenings reveal what's hidden deep in the multitrack mix. Some of the humor of troupe members Phillip Austin, Peter Bergman, David Ossman, and Phillip Proctor is hopelessly, charmingly dated—especially the innocent drug references—but this is one of the few records of this ilk that offers more with every listening. Also worth searching out, and almost up to this level, are *Don't Touch That Dwarf Hand Me the Pliers*, in which the aliens turn out to be us; *How Can You Be in Two Places When You're Not Anywhere at All*, about time travel and Raymond Chandler; and *Forward into the Past*, a two-LP compilation.

Number Fifty-Two

Sly and the Family Stone
There's a Riot Goin' On
Epic, 1971

The party always ends, the drugs take their toll, and things fall apart. In the late sixties, thanks to their spirited records and their filmed performance at Woodstock, Sylvester Stewart and his San Francisco band the Family Stone epitomized optimistic egalitarianism. Their greatest hits— "Dance to the Music," "Everyday People," "Stand!," and "Thank You (Falettine Be Mice Elf Agin)"—were as celebratory and openhearted as any in pop music. These were songs about unlimited possibility for oneself and tolerance for others; these were love songs in dozens of ways.

Sly's drug problems were transforming him into something of an unsure show on the arena scene (among major performers, only George "No-Show" Jones earned a worse reputation), and the physical and spiritual dissatisfaction such habits represented were a major part of his 1971 album *There's a Riot Goin' On.* Sly was far from the end of his rope—subsequent records suggest that he could find nooses in all corners—but it was clear that Sly's intention was to make a record that was nothing so much unexpected as off-putting. Yet he accomplished both. Desolation and anger, sadnesses triumphed over in his earlier albums, were at the core of *There's a Riot Goin' On,* and coming from someone known for his ability to dance over all sorrows, the record shook many listeners awake. And although the LP peaked at Number One, it also scared many away.

The deliberate beats underline the sense of violation of *Theres a Riot Goin' On:* Basses burp at odd intervals, drums stumble and stutter, and rhythm guitars sometimes drop out of the mix completely. The big hit from the record, "Family Affair," at least partly a play on the name of the band, provided a perfect extended metaphor for the sorrow and ravages that Sly suddenly recognized around him. His shouts before the fade, a brief arousal from his sad stupor, sound like the cries Al Green was perfecting a continent away, but this was the dark side of Green's romantic longing. There was nothing warm about the performance: "Nobody wants to be left out" was its key slurred line. Even more muddy, moving, and ominous was "Thank You for Talkin' to Me Africa," a downer remake of "Thank You (Falettine Be Mice Elf Agin)" that remains incredibly influential to this day in its call to address untouched issues in unexpected ways, no matter the costs (it cost Sly his career). Bands like Public Enemy and N.W.A. are this scary only in their dreams.

Number Fifty-Three

Michael Jackson
Off the Wall
Epic, 1979

Why has this record, which sold a mere eight million units, lasted better than *Thriller*, the most popular album in the history of recorded music? Superficially, it's because of the violation by Michael Jackson of the amazing love nearly all lovers of pop music felt for the former child star in that heady period between his performance of "Billie Jean" on the *Motown 25* television special and the Don King-supervised announcement of the *Victory* tour that started the unfixable rupture in the Gloved One's crown. The rote dates on the *Victory* tour and, more than that, Jackson's reaction to the ramifications of his megasuccess let us down so much that it resulted in a backlash against the music.

But that's not why *Thriller* doesn't peak as high or as often as its predecessor, *Off the Wall*. The truth is in the grooves: The greatness of *Thriller* is based on a mere three outstanding cuts—"Wanna Be Startin' Somethin'," "Billie Jean," and "Beat It," all forward-looking masterpieces that Jackson will probably never surpass. But much of the rest of the record is lightweight—"The Girl Is Mine," a duet with the former rocker Paul McCartney, is so flimsy it evaporates before the first of its profoundly annoying choruses. What was brilliant on *Thriller* was unprecedented stuff; but there wasn't enough of it to sustain the entire LP.

That's not the case with *Off the Wall*, the 1979 album that served as Jackson's declaration of independence from the Motown production mill that had begun to strangle him, as it had many other gifted performers before him. It also remains—with the exception of his three breakthrough cuts on *Thriller*—the only time he has presented himself believably as an adult. (This was long before his companions were more likely to be animals or child actors who were unlikely to truly challenge him as

104

a human being.) The record is full of phenomenally sensual, even sexual, performances, from the "You make me feel like . . . You make me feel like . . . Woo!" explosion that kicks off "Don't Stop 'Til You Get Enough" to Jackson's triumph over conventionality in the final "Burn This Disco Out."

In terms of willful taboo violations, Jackson is of course no Prince, whose contemporaneous *Dirty Mind* expanded funk and rock into territory that would make even Jerry Lee Lewis blush, but Jackson brought to *Off the Wall* vocal tricks that no pop singer, before or after, could have imagined. His tenor flies all over the place (even semi-rapping a bit on "Get on the Floor"), but the most expressive vocal moments here are wordless—cries, shouts, exultations, sighs that speak volumes. There's minimal artifice here, and not merely because Jackson had not begun his tabloid-intensive, self-destructive addiction to plastic surgery. "She's Out of My Life" is a believable ballad about the breakup of a long-term relationship from a man who claims he has never had one, and producer Quincy Jones helps Jackson speak clearly and wildly without resorting to the smooth tricks that clutter *Thriller, Bad,* and the other ten thousand records Jones has produced since *Off the Wall.* Jackson's emotions triumph over his image on *Off the Wall,* and for more than any reason that's why this record is his most essential.

Number Fifty-Four

The Drifters
Let the Boogie Woogie Roll:
Greatest Hits: 1953–1958
All Time Greatest Hits and More:
1959–1965
Atlantic, 1988

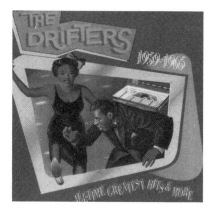

These two double records (each with half a dozen extra tracks in its compact-disc configuration) present the definitive collections of the Drifters, one of pop's most lasting and elastic vocal units. *Let the Boogie Woogie Roll* concentrates on the period in which Clyde McPhatter was the group's defiant lead singer, and it presents a primal but polished vocal quartet. Shepherded by Ahmet Ertegun and Jerry Wexler, the group expanded on blues singing and arrangement conventions with such vigor and such ease that it sounded like they were creating something brand new with each cut like "The Way I Feel" and "Such a Night." Toward the end of this set, Ertegun and Wexler give way to producers and writers Jerry Leiber and Mike Stoller, who promptly transformed the group into a devastatingly effective pop unit. Along with Ray Charles, they built the bridge from rhythm and blues to pop.

On *All Time Greatest Hits and More*, Leiber and Stoller worked with a variety of trenchant-minded lead vocalists, among them Ben E. King, Johnny Williams, Johnny Moore, and Rudy Lewis, but with the group's personnel changing so quickly, what mattered most were the believable-romantic songs and the lush arrangements. And what songs they were!: "There Goes My Baby," "Save the Last Dance for Me," "Up on the Roof," "On Broadway," "Under the Boardwalk," and on and on. All the singers sounded as if they believed their myths, essential in attracting listeners of all ages. Leiber and Stoller's songs rang true to both the puppy-love and silver-anniversary crowds. These two double-albums are about clashes of forms, conflicts of sophistication and gutbucket. They tell the story of the birth of a new form, and they are never less than spectacular.

Number Fifty-Five

Huey "Piano" Smith
Rock 'n' Roll Revival
Ace, 1975

"Gooba, gooba, gooba, gooba! Ah, ah, ah ah ah!" New Orleans rhythm and blues is known for its rolling rhythms and a "soon come" attitude to life that rivals the cheerful fatalism of Rastafarian music. Except for some Little Richard workouts, most of the notable workouts from New Orleans took their good time, letting us dance along with the band, not wearing anybody out too quickly—so the party could go on all night.

Although Antoine "Fats" Domino and some of Dave Bartholemew's accompanists are better known, the definitive New Orleans pianist was Huey "Piano" Smith. (Little Richard was a great pianist, but he was many things before that. And truth be told, Smith played piano on some Little Richard sessions.) Smith's lolling style, as a player, writer, and arranger, was his most distinguishing characteristic. He wasn't the world's greatest singer—many of the late fifties singles that cohere on *Rock 'n' Roll Revival* feature other singers before Smith's piano and crack rhythm section—but he was a genius manipulator of talent. How else to explain how he took an unstudied pretty boy like Frankie Ford and got him to sound like a wise rhythm-and-blues vet? Worth seeking out is Ford's *Let's Take a Sea Cruise*, which includes both his hits and "Roberta," in which Ford is unable to pawn his girlfriend of that name because she won't (can't?) sign her name. The Ford cut here, "Alimony," is a remarkably adult tune about intermittent child-support payments, pushed across by a rollicking beat that makes thirty days in the pen sound like fun.

On this record Smith takes over lead vocal in his own version of the hit he wrote and produced for Ford, "Sea Cruise," featuring brilliant throw-away/profound lines like "I got the boogie-woogie like a knife in the back" (an extension of the idea behind the classic two-part "Rockin'

107

Pneumonia and the Boogie Woogie Flu''). Smith loved these tossed-off lines; one of them—''You got me rockin' when I ought to be rollin'''— he appreciated so much that he stuffed it into two songs, ''Don't You Just Know It'' and ''Little Liza Jane.'' Throughout the record, such delight keeps jutting out of the mix. Some might consider *Rock 'n' Roll Revival* some sort of New Orleans various-performers greatest-hits set, but it's really a testament to one wild man's beautiful vision.

Number Fifty-Six

Iron City Houserockers
Have a Good Time (But Get Out Alive)
MCA, 1980

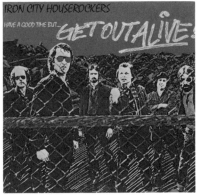

When punk crested on these shores, it was hard for a decidedly old-wave bar band to be heard as anything other than a throwback. Journeymen like the Iron City Houserockers had to get smarter. If their concern for workaday disillusions and fleeting escape through the pickup-truck radio wasn't exactly anarchy in motion, they had to show potential trend-setting fans nationwide that it wasn't just low-budget arena pomp, either. And the Iron City Houserockers pulled it off.

Have a Good Time (But Get Out Alive), the second of the Pittsburgh sextet's four albums, is fierce and admonishing. In songs like "Don't Let Them Push You Around," "Pumping Iron," and "We're Not Dead Yet," singer and guitarist Joe Grushecky's raging chronicles of commonplace urban loss tumble amidst an avalanche of guitars. No surprise there: The album was produced by guitar-rock kings Ian Hunter and Mick Ronson.

In "Blondie," long-time fan Grushecky tells of saving up for scalped tickets and feels betrayed that "Now they're playing your song in all those places/That won't let me and Angela in." This was the first, and still about the only, rock-and-roll song to explicitly question the merchandising of "new wave" to the paying customers.

Cutting deeper are the pairing of "Old Man Bar" and "Junior's Bar." In the slow, deliberate "Old Man Bar," pianist Gil Snyder growls out the tale of a young steelworker listening to World War II veterans repeating battle tales; in the "Junior's Bar" treatment, over the same melody, Grushecky is at another tavern, desperate to connect, terrified to make a move. All these characters—steelworkers, retirees, bank robbers, dole walkers, drunks—end up crushed, muttering warnings for those about to

109

face the wheel. This bloodied defiance linked the Iron City Houserockers to punk; it also suggested that the mainstream didn't have to be the home of the spayed anymore.

Number Fifty-Seven

Johnny Horton
The World of Johnny Horton
Columbia, 1966

Johnny Horton is a cult figure. Perhaps he isn't revered as a first-rate country performer, which he was, because he never settled into a single mode. As with his friend Johnny Cash, it was hard to get a handle on him. Horton's crossover hits were semi-satiric, historical narratives like "The Battle of New Orleans," "Sink the Bismarck," and the grisly murder remembrance "When It's Springtime in Alaska," and he was clearly dedicated to scoring hits from sentimental patriotic tributes like "Johnny Freedom" and "Young Abe Lincoln." But on occasion, he slipped in a honky-tonk (or rockabilly) gut-buster.

Befitting country-and-western convention, Horton sported an Everyman voice—pinched range but directness and fervor in the notes he could reach. His well-mannered affability is sometimes a liability—his attack on Hank Williams's "Lost Highway" misses most of the tune's despair—but usually his unworried, unstudied singing lets the listener concentrate on the song narrative.

Horton's least novelty-like, and thus most enduring, hits are "I'm Ready, If You're Willing," an anxious shuffle, the romantic, wishful "Honky Tonk Man" (covered magnificently by Dwight Yoakam in a version that launched his career), and "I'm Coming Home," a 1957 tale of a truck driver returning to the hearth that is perhaps the greatest advertisement for sex in a country song not performed by Jerry Lee Lewis, although it was oblique enough to have been a hit. Horton died in a 1960 car crash he was said to have prophesied. His widow is Billy Jean Horton, formerly the second Mrs. Hank Williams.

The World of Johnny Horton suffers from that abomination noted in the small print that warns "electronically re-recorded to simulate stereo," an

111

earlier era's misguided equivalent of the "colorization" of black-and-white films. Remember to flick the mono switch. For those who want more, this set has been superseded by a four-CD set from Bear Family that contains every single one of Horton's Columbia recordings and features a stupendous biographical booklet by Colin Escott.

Number Fifty-Eight

Merle Haggard
*A Tribute to the Best Damn Fiddle
Player in the World (Or, My
Salute to Bob Wills)*
Capitol, 1970

This one is stone country but merits inclusion for its very rock-and-roll-like defiance, energy, and audacity.

The finest country performers are often those who are most haunted by tradition and spend the most time struggling with their places in it. (Same in rock and roll. Ever heard of Bruce Springsteen?) Haggard has recorded several tribute LPs (*The Way It Was in '51* to Hank Williams and Lefty Frizzell, *Same Train, a Different Time* to Jimmie Rodgers, and *My Farewell to Elvis*), but this is the one that is most clearly a celebration rather than a vanity project.

Haggard reassembled original members of Bob Wills's Texas Playboys and led them through a dozen Western swing classics either written by or closely associated with Wills. The selections testify to both the lasting vitality and the stubborn consistency of the bold jazz/country-and-western hybrid that Wills popularized and thus forever broadened ideas about country's flexibility.

On this record, Haggard can't fiddle to save his neck—he'd only been playing the instrument for three months when he recorded *Tribute*—and his narration over "Brown Skinned Gal" is more than a bit mawkish, but these are fleeting problems. It's Haggard's dark, full-of-fear-and-longing voice, not his fiddling, that leads the band, and sentimentality has always lived in country's heart. Moreover, the weepers here stomp, and the stompers weep. There have been innumerable country labors of love, and this is one of the few that has verve equal to its respect.

Number Fifty-Nine

The Everly Brothers
Roots
Warner Brothers, 1968

Going back to songs they had known all their lives had worked once on *Songs Our Daddy Taught Us,* so why not again, especially at a time when the Everly Brothers' career was in collapse? The harmony brothers were desperate in 1968. They'd only scored one chart single in the past four years, and they hadn't broken the Top Ten since 1962. They'd cracked it with a junky song, too.

All this didn't matter. *Roots* doesn't sound like a last stand; many of the songs fit together like shaking hands. The whole record, from the recognizable but not too obvious selection of country standards to the home-made 1952 family tapes that frame it, seems meticulously considered. Part of the credit goes to Warner Brothers staff producer Lenny Waronker, who for once gave Don and Phil the freedom to record straight country and schmaltz-free country-pop.

The brothers rose to the occasion. They had no trouble with their struggles to find out how to be "contemporary," when they had undeniable material like Merle Haggard's "Mama Tried" and "Sing Me Back Home," and Jimmie Rodgers's "T for Texas." They were uneasy at first, but they let their harmonies draw closer and closer until they bounced, achieving a friendly performance they could no longer hope to pull off otherwise. The Everly Brothers would not make music this formidable for another fifteen years, and *Roots* was such a bomb it didn't even enter *Billboard*'s pop album chart, but it stands as the duo's only mid-period work in which they offered to each other or their audience something worth sharing: lived-in history. The innocence of their early hits was gone (although I'll argue to my grave that the relationship in "Wake Up Little Suzie" was a sexual one), replaced with a wisdom that sounded earned.

Number Sixty

Graham Parker
Heat Treatment
Mercury, 1976

If you think you're bashing your head against the wall with your work, consider Graham Parker's predicament. The London singer broke away from the murky British pub scene with a pair of scalding rhythm-and-punk records and a band (the Rumour, also edgy pub-rock vets) that put across Parker's agitated yet human vision with the concision of the Stax house band. At their early best, Parker and the Rumour suggested Van Morrison fronting an angrier, more sober version of the Faces. But both these early albums, *Howlin' Wind* and *Heat Treatment,* stiffed, and with few meaningful exceptions Parker is still met with industry and audience indifference.

Out of nowhere, Parker appeared in 1976 with an almost cathartic commitment to direct expression, and an attitude right out of punk. *Howlin' Wind,* the debut, mixed sixties soul with British reggae stylings on songs like "Don't Ask Me Questions," in which the diminutive singer argued with everyone from his friends to God and gave and received no quarter from any of his targets. *Heat Treatment,* which came out a few months later, seemed at first to be a lighter work, with a few hey-baby-let's-party songs and an ode to a hotel chambermaid, but repeated listenings reveal it as an expansion on sources so global and incongruous it's amazing they fit on the same album.

For every line anticipating destruction ("You wind up eating all the friends you found" as well as the everything-is-disintegrating rhetoric you'd expect from someone allied with the punks), there are hundreds that add up to an uncompromising rant against cynicism, a snarl that won't get out of your face. These never deteriorate into the easy vice of nihilism, primarily because the Rumour and accompanying horn section are intent on drawing out the traditional elements in all the songs. Epics of lost possibility like "That's What They All Say" and "Turned Up Too Late" turn on the clipped rhythms of guitarists Brinsley Schwarz and Martin Belmont, and Robert John Lange's low-key production rounds some edges but leaves others hanging in the wind, especially in the *Moondance*-derived ballads.

When Parker is finally comfortable showing the dream behind his anger—particularly on his statement of purpose, "Fools' Gold," the last song on the album—he makes all the elements whole. Parker has subsequently recorded one more great album (1979's *Squeezing Out Sparks*) and several other good ones, but it was on *Heat Treatment* that he married his love for rock and roll and his distrust of the world that spawned it.

Number Sixty-One

La Vern Baker
Real Gone Gal
Charly, 1984

La Vern Baker could and did sing just about anything, which was partly why the Atlantic Records soul singer never became a superstar. She was as comfortable with blues shouting (1953's "How Can You Leave a Man Like This") as she was with straight rock ("Hey Memphis," from 1961, a pungent reworking of Elvis Presley's "Little Sister"), gnarly rhythm-and-blues (the 1958 hit "Voodoo Voodoo"), or soulful, saxophone-driven ballads (1955's "My Happiness Forever").

Baker was solidly in the Bessie Smith tradition (she even recorded a tribute record to her obvious inspiration) in that she was a singer with enough power to break a song in two and with enough smarts to ride the rhythms gently when appropriate. But Baker was all over the place with her material at a time when rhythm-and-blues singers and pop warblers were different species with wildly disparate agendas. Baker's few attempts at light material ("Tweedle Dee" and "Tra La La," neither included on *Real Gone Gal*) often had their thunder stolen by vapid cover-version specialist Georgia Gibbs, and it's no accident that Baker's lone Top Ten pop smash, "I Cried a Tear" (Number Six in 1959), suggests a mere marketing gesture.

But Baker could surely take charge of songs associated with other performers. She grabbed Faye Adams's "Shake a Hand" and slowed down the tempo so much that the communal rapture of the original turned into a desperate plea to be noticed. And isn't the ability to make a popular song one's own a prime yardstick for measuring a singer's greatness?

Number Sixty-Two

The Temptations
Anthology
Motown, 1986

Motown's *Anthology* series of greatest-hits collections was full of hit-or-miss propositions, especially the compact disc versions, which extended stories past virtually everyone's prime. Most of the label's top acts were single-oriented groups (Stevie Wonder and Marvin Gaye being major exceptions) and over the course of fifty-odd songs their tics and sameness grated on all but the most devoted listeners. The Temptations' installment in the series goes on a bit too long, which means that only thirty-five of its forty-two songs are fantastic.

The extraordinary achievements of the Temptations are best measured by the distance from their first Number One, 1965's "My Girl," to their last, 1972's "Papa Was a Rollin' Stone." (I'll stay away from biography since Vince Aletti's notes to the set are definitive.) Their early sound, as epitomized by "My Girl," was the most innocent of the great Motown vocal groups, at least partly because their primary songwriter and occasional producer was Smokey Robinson, the master of innocent-minded soul. They sang of sunshine on a cloudy day and provided it, and made sweet nothings sound like essential truths. But by the time they recorded the courageous "Papa Was a Rollin' Stone," by which time their major producer and writer was Norman Whitfield, the world had changed. Except for Marvin Gaye and Stevie Wonder's genre-shattering work of the time, this is the most self-consciously experimental single ever cut at Motown, and one of the best, all 6:53 of it. Ominous bass and cymbals, elliptical strings, and a guitar from the set of *Shaft* frame the story of abandoned familial love with such intensity and determination that pop music still hasn't caught up to it, not even after the hundreds of soundalike pieces that emerged in the wake of its breakthrough success. It wasn't

118

merely that the song took on hard issues with sophistication, but that the song's sophistication was outstripped only by its power.

There are dozens more amazing songs here—"Get Ready," "Ain't Too Proud To Beg," "I Wish It Would Rain," and 1971's anachronistic "Just My Imagination"—but the road from "My Girl" to "Papa Was a Rolling Stone" ran parallel to devastating changes in culture that no one could make sense of, and the Temptations were among the few who could even document it.

Number Sixty-Three

Various Performers
The Complete Million Dollar Session
Charly, 1987

December 4, 1956: Carl Perkins was searching for a hit, Jerry Lee Lewis was playing piano for him, and company showed up. As Perkins's session began to wind down, the reception area in front of the studio crowded. Johnny Cash walked in unannounced, along with his wife Vivian and their eighteen-month-old daughter Rosanne. Someone opened the door between the reception area and the studio, and the session turned into a party. Then Elvis Presley, the most famous man in the Western world, arrived with a showgirl named Marilyn Evans, arguably the only positive aspect of his first, otherwise disastrous, appearance in Las Vegas. Cash smiled for the newspaper cameras and left to shop. The crowd moved into the studio and Jack Clement kept the tapes rolling.

Jerry Lee, Carl, and Elvis had all turned to a music career to avoid the dead ends they sensed elsewhere—none of them wanted to relive his father's life—but they embraced music in the first place because it was a mystery they could love, explore, and through their pursuits find more reasons to love. All of them first discovered music in church, so it is no surprise that the common ground they found when they started harmonizing was sacred music. Jerry Lee's mother damned him for playing secular music, Carl sang about knife fights, and Elvis had been called everything short of the antichrist, but gospel was what they instinctively chose. Fluid, fervent versions of songs like "When God Dips His Love in My Heart," "Just a Little Talk with Jesus," "Down by the Riverside," and "Blessed Jesus Hold My Hand" jumped out of them in a relaxed, spontaneous rush. Perkins's band supplied the artless accompaniment, and even Marilyn Evans joined in. The song selection gradually drifted to hits of the day, among them Charlie Singleton's "Don't Forbid Me," which noted antirock singer Pat Boone had just defanged in a cover version. Elvis said that the song had been written for him, that an acetate of it had been "over my house for ages, man. I never did see it, so much junk lyin' around."

Talk turned to Chuck Berry, their fellow performer and songwriter whose work all of them treasured. They played multiple snatches of Berry's "Too Much Monkey Business" and "Brown-Eyed Handsome Man" until they got the words right and then argued which song was better. The trio sang the rockabilly anthem "Rip It Up," Elvis enjoying an alternate version of its first line: "It's Saturday night and I just got paid, uh, laid." These were priceless moments, an opportunity for a man to jettison the sex-symbol nonsense and just play. For a long time this session was known as the Million Dollar Quartet, but even marked down twenty-five percent as the result of Cash's absence (it was first thought that he had participated in the jam), this was a bargain.

Elvis was cordial, but he had to move on. In singles and pairs, everyone skedaddled until only Jerry Lee remained. "How'd it go?" his cousin Myra asked him when he returned to her home late that night.

Number Sixty-Four

Etta James
Tell Mama
Chess, 1968

Conventional wisdom, the greatest disease caused by the complacency that afflicts ninety percent of all rock critics, states that the great rhythm-and-blues singer Jamesetta Hawkins, a.k.a. Etta James, never recorded an album as massive as her talents. As usual, such conventional wisdom is grounded in an iota of fact and then turns out to be completely wrong, i.e., a lie.

As it did with all of its female singers, Chess Records had much trouble placing James. They tried her out on big-band ballads, straight blues, and the uptempo rhythm-and-blues hits with which she had scored in the fifties, like "Dance with Me Henry." But no matter what the style, she wasn't generating any hits, though many individual tracks were sinewy and harrowing (cf. the compilations *Peaches* and *The Sweetest Peaches*).

Producer Rick Hall believed in James enough to fly her down to Fame Studios, in Muscle Shoals, Alabama, a place where soul smashes were being cut every day, it seemed. The idea was to get a rough, smoldering album out of her—very much in the mode of Aretha Franklin, who had recently broken out of a similar rut with churchy soul. The result, *Tell Mama*, is the only soul-bandwagon record that can stand with Lady Soul's classics from the period.

The big rhythm-and-blues hit was the Clarence Carter title track, a compressed explosion of affirmation and generosity. The acknowledged standard is "I'd Rather Go Blind," in which James takes standard better-dead-than-unloved banalities and exposes them as true. Turn the volume as low as you like; she'll still overtake everyone in a crowded room. Even the album's giving songs sound generated by hurt; James sings as if she knows that alleviating someone else's sorrow won't lessen her load one bit.

Number Sixty-Five

James Carr
You Got My Mind Messed Up
Goldwax, 1966

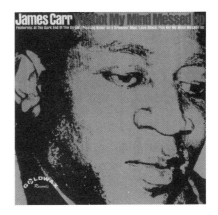

Once upon a time, even when Otis was alive and Aretha mattered, James Carr was the world's greatest soul singer. In the late sixties, Carr was without peer, a penetrating vocalist whose greatest hits—"You've Got My Mind Messed Up," "Pouring Water on a Drowning Man," and "The Dark End of the Street"—showed him off as one of the few top-rank singers of the era who didn't record for Stax or Motown (he recorded for Stax's little sister in Memphis, Goldwax). His voice was among soul's darkest and most demon-driven; it's no exaggeration to consider him the soul equivalent of Robert Johnson. Also like Johnson, Carr could sing any type of pop music. Aside from his masterful soul sides, he also committed definitive versions of songs as diverse as the Bee Gee's "To Love Somebody" and Harlan Howard's country smash "Life Turned Her That Way."

"He could have been the greatest," Jim Dickinson, the Memphis producer and musician who did some sessions with Carr in the late sixties, told me in mid-1991. "He had the greatest R&B voice I've ever been in the room with, and I've worked with Sam and Dave and Brook Benton. It's a stretch, but I think James's voice was better than Otis Redding's. It was more emotional. Otis had a frenzy in his voice that James didn't, but James's was up from the church in a way Otis's never was."

Carr's fan club included Aretha Franklin, who used his recording of "The Dark End of the Street" as the basis for her own remarkable version. Yet after a relatively brief (1966–1969) period of chart success, by all accounts Carr fell apart. Some blamed drugs, but what truly haunted Carr was a profound, lengthy bout with depression. Even in his heyday, Carr was often accompanied in the studio by a nurse. His behavior became more erratic and his recordings became far less frequent. Carr was briefly managed by Phil Walden and Duane Allman, blew deals with several labels, and in 1979 hit bottom during a makeshift Japanese tour when he froze up onstage. As reported by Peter Guralnick in *Sweet Soul Music,* the James Carr of the early eighties was barely conscious, unkempt, devoid of all but the most rudimentary reality testing. "There were times when I just couldn't reach him," acknowledges Quinton Claunch, one of the founders of Goldwax. It seemed the sad end of a once seemingly limitless career.

In 1990, Carr recorded a new record that came within shouting distance of his greatest performances. On the record, he is aided by some of his most crucial Goldwax colleagues: producers Claunch, whose credits go back to his days at Sun Records playing bass with Carl Perkins, and Roosevelt Jamison, whose two decades of commitment to Carr have led him to such extremes as mortgaging his home to buy studio time for James. The record wasn't great, but its release was an excuse for me to learn more about the artist.

Carr, now fifty-one, has lived for years in South Memphis with one of his sisters. Sitting in a hotel room just outside Memphis, accompanied by Claunch and Goldwax director Elliott Clark, Carr has his own agenda. He snaps his long fingernails, intently peruses the covers of some of his old records (I happen to have a few with me), and needs a long time with a newcomer before he is comfortable enough to talk. It is startling that it is so difficult to draw out even the most elementary responses from the commanding vocalist. But even when he says, "I'm doing the best I can. It's all I can do," in his low, quiet, rough voice, one can hear a hint of the dark tremble that makes his singing voice so unique. One does not have to go far to find the source of the deep emotion that anchors all Carr's records.

Carr lightens up a bit when he gets a chance to list his favorite singers. "I like the old folks," he says, and points to Sam Cooke, Clyde McPhatter, Little Milton, Bobby Bland, the Soul Stirrers, the Dixie Hummingbirds, and the Five Blind Boys of Alabama as crucial influences. Not surprisingly, most of the performers are sacred singers. Before his solo success, Carr sang with a gospel group called the Harmony Echoes, and Claunch insists that Carr could "cut a fantastic gospel album. That's where his heart is." Carr slowly nods his approval.

But don't ask Carr to look forward. He treats any questions about the future as if they signal something ominous. "I'm in the slums. Sometimes

I'm ashamed of myself, I don't know. I am a different person from the James Carr that toured with Otis Redding. I'm out of shape. I was in better shape. Not much, but better. I'm not sure I want to keep singing, but I'm not done yet. At least I've accomplished something. I'm more tuned in than I used to be." He smiles, knowing his return is no simple triumph.

Carr is extremely dependent on the perseverance of men like Clark, Claunch, and Jamison, yet he wouldn't submit himself to the pressures of recording and promoting if he didn't have the strength, or the will. "Singing is all I can do," he says softly and deliberately. "Singing is business, but it makes life worth living."

Number Sixty-Six

Al Green
Call Me
Hi, 1972

Soul music can mean anything you want it to, especially if you're Al Green. Before he gave up in 1980, the greatest soul singer of the seventies (not merely because there was no competition left) mixed all sorts of traditions—blues, country, pop, the Beatles' "I Want To Hold Your Hand," rural gospel—and came up with a unique gumbo that continued the tradition that began with Arthur Alexander and reached its apotheosis in the studios of Stax Records. Indeed, although Green was born in Arkansas, he recorded in Memphis, and he was the clear inheritor of the mantle Otis Redding wore at Stax, as well as someone who could add new accoutrements to that cape.

Green produced his records with Hi Records executive Willie Mitchell, and together they summoned up staccato horns, pumping strings, and a light-but-insistent rhythm section over which Green's transfiguring improvisations could dance. Virtually all of Green's albums before he turned to Jesus full-time are spectacular—special note should be given *Let's Stay Together* and *The Belle Album,* as well as many recent compilations—but *Call Me* is unequivocally Green's most towering achievement, the album on which his eccentric voice and his eccentric tastes coalesced most spectacularly. Seven of its nine cuts are Green originals, among them his most explicit devotional song to that point and several cuts ("Call Me," "Here I Am," "You Ought to Be with Me") that remain among his most carnal. The other two are classic country songs, Hank Williams's "I'm So Lonely I Could Cry" and Willie Nelson's "Funny How Time Slips Away," devastated country-soul fusions that are very much of a piece with the rest of the album. The beat unifies all, and not in typical disco lowest-common-denominator fashion; the steadiness lets emotions soar free.

126

Number Sixty-Seven

Buddy Holly
The Complete Buddy Holly
MCA, 1979

It's probably not fair for me to drop a six-record set of an artist's complete works into this selection, but the fact is that Buddy Holly's talents justify the treatment. It's impossible to leave anything out. Holly was only twenty-two when his plane went down over Mason City, Iowa (though, compared to fellow passenger Ritchie Valens, he was a grizzled veteran), and simply wasn't around long enough to fall apart, as every major rock-and-roll performer does sooner or later. Revisionists may claim that Holly would have eventually turned into a middle-of-the-road crooner, but the one hundred and eighteen cuts here (plus interviews) are evidence of a still-growing talent that had yet to wimp out. Unlike too many aficionados of the form, let's stick to the music.

Holly came of musical age while Elvis Presley was recording for Sun. As sophisticated as Holly and the Crickets were to be able to maneuver themselves in their relatively short time together, Holly's greatest dream was to become Elvis. I don't necessarily mean that Holly wanted Elvis's fame, although what eighteen-year-old wouldn't? What Holly wanted most of all was Elvis's touch, the ability to be a bluesman, a country strummer, and something brand new all at the same time. Throughout Holly's tragically brief career, he touched on all areas, determined to wrap his warm, hiccuping voice around everything, from rockabilly standards to softer tunes like "It Doesn't Matter Anymore," perhaps the only instance of a great version of a song written by Paul Anka.

Holly's genius was to dream his Elvis dream, internalize it, and then figure out how Buddy Holly could be better than Elvis. Of course he wasn't, but anyone in rock and roll who isn't convinced that he or she can become the best in the field had better find a new way to pay the rent.

127

Whereas most people in rock and roll are convinced that they already are the greatest (fill in the blank) the world has ever seen, only the true searchers are smart enough to know that they're not there yet but confident enough to insist that they have a chance.

Holly didn't surpass Elvis as a singer or bandleader, but Buddy had something on his role model: He could write. Anyone who wrote "That'll Be the Day," "It's So Easy," "I'm Lookin' for Someone to Love," "Peggy Sue" (source of the greatest rhythm guitar solo in all rock and roll), "Words of Love," "Well . . . All Right," "Think It Over," and "True Love Ways" over the course of a long career would have an impressive catalog; Holly was only starting. Holly's specialty was midtempo rock and roll, a bit softer than the rockabilly cuts, but still with an edge. Songs like "Oh Boy!" and "Rock Around With Ollie Vee" were occasions for Holly to shout, plead, laugh, and swing his way through expressions of optimism about the future that nothing could derail. *The Complete Buddy Holly* showcases the work of the friendliest performer in rock and roll, and one of the few smiling rockers who had a brain.

Of course, *The Complete Buddy Holly* didn't turn out to be everything. Several LPs of outtakes and alternate takes have emerged, some of them through legal means. I recommend them all.

Number Sixty-Eight

The Four Tops
Second Album
Motown, 1965

One of the articles of faith that led me to write this book is that albums are not merely collections of singles. If that were the case, every record in this book would be someone or another's *Greatest Hits* or *Best of.* That's why there are so few early Motown LPs here, although many of the early Temptations, Miracles, Supremes, Four Tops, and Vandellas albums offered music as lively and aware as any committed to a mastering lathe in the early sixties. The Four Tops were not even the finest of those groups, but they were the only one that presented an early original album that added up to more than the sum of its parts. The title of the Four Tops' *Second Album* suggests how little thought Motown gave to albums, which makes its success as a unit that much more impressive.

The Four Tops were the most experienced group to land at Motown, having formed in 1953 and recorded for Chess soon thereafter. They had no success there or at Red Top or Columbia, and they arrived at Motown decade-old veterans, ancient compared to the kids working through Berry Gordy's charm school. Their first album made a bit of noise ("Baby I Need Your Loving" just missed the Top Ten), but it wasn't until the sessions for their second album that the Four Tops and their producers, Brian Holland and Lamont Dozier (two-thirds of the Holland-Dozier-Edward Holland team that wrote so many of the Four Tops' and others' early hits) figured out what they were after in the teen-soul sweepstakes.

Four Tops records were characterized by lead vocalist Levi Stubbs overemoting so much he became believable again, buttressed by falsetto background vocals and the slippery James Jamerson/Benny Benjamin rhythm section that made even the pleas ("I Can't Help Myself" and "It's the Same Old Song" are lonely demands for affection) sound like fun. It's no surprise that as these songs and those of other early Motown groups have become popular again, most people respond to the propulsive beat and forget (or choose to forget) the consternation, even terror, at the core of these songs. Thanks for nothing, *Big Chill.*

Second Album explodes out of the gate with "I Can't Help Myself," but all twelve of its love songs demand equal attention. It's no surprise that the ostensibly happy love songs on the record aren't quite convincing; this is a group, after all, that thrives on the contradiction of smiling through the most downhearted compositions. So the truest cut on *Second Album* is no doubt the supple, mystical "Love Feels Like Fire." Stop-and-start harmonies dance around Stubbs, singing "Love's made a happy man of me" in describing his happiness, but what kind of image is fire to summon up bliss? This complex ambivalence is a fundamental part of the attraction of the Four Tops, an extremely important element that most listeners and critics prefer to ignore.

Number Sixty-Nine

Johnny Cash
The Sun Years
Rhino, 1990

Johnny Cash's Sun years have gotten the full treatment they deserve, first in a complete Charly LP box and then in a more complete Bear Family CD set called The Man in Black but this single disc for once does an almost unbeatable job of summarizing one of Sun's greatest artists. There are a few major deletionsany Cash compilation without "Cry Cry Cry" has a strike against it, but I'd much rather you spend the dough on James Brown and Carl Perkins boxed sets so I'll leave you to just this one record.

Cash is legendary in country circles, but the rock-and-roll audience often diminishes his talents by claiming that his early songs "all sound the same," usually pointing to the boom-chicka-boom sound he developed with guitarist Luther Perkins and bassist Marshall Grant as the culprit. The beat that this Tennessee Three discovered was far more malleable than its detractors maintain (it should also be noted that the beat did begin wavering, but not until long after Cash moved on to Columbia, and even then not all the time). Cash's boom-chicka-boom was the bluesiest of country beats, mimicking the rhythms of the trains that plowed through so many of Cash's songs, and giving the tunes a sense of openness often discouraged (or, at the least, difficult to achieve) in Sun's cluttered Union Avenue studio.

Seventeen of the eighteen cuts on *The Sun Years* were originally singles, and as such the set concentrates on the side of Cash that the artist and producer Jack Clement most wanted to present to the world. That's why a soda-pop number like "Ballad of a Teenage Queen," an attempt to stuff the obviously country Cash into a teen-idol suit, is here. But Cash held sway in the studio and on this collection; only three songs here are written by others.

Cash the writer understood Cash the singer, and that singer knew better than any producer or A&R representative how to employ his dark baritone. Bare-boned songs like "Folsom Prison Blues," "Hey Porter," "I Walk the Line," "Get Rhythm," and "Train of Love" anticipated future marriages of hard country and hard rock; these numbers call on the unswayable rhythms of the rails to carry tales of fidelity, regret, adventure, and most often all at the same time, with such lines as "Everyone's baby but mine's comin' home" and "I shot a man in Reno just to watch him die." Cash bought all the myths of honky tonk, but he knew that Elvis had changed the world, and he tried to find himself a home in it. And in "Come In Stranger," the phenomenally erotic tale of a country singer like Cash being welcomed home after a long haul on the road, all the contradictions come together and add up to a complex life worth hearing about. *The Sun Years* is only the beginning of Cash's great story, but it does suggest nearly all of the high points ahead.

Number Seventy

Rockpile
Seconds of Pleasure
Columbia, 1980

It's hard to make great simple rock and roll, especially when you've got a fertile mind. It might be even harder when you're blessed with two diverse minds. Songwriter and bassist Nick Lowe produced decisive early albums by Graham Parker and Elvis Costello, and his two late-seventies LPs, *Pure Pop for Now People* (known in the U.K. as *Jesus of Cool*) and *Labour of Lust,* were hardy, side-splitting records that exemplified how humor and trenchant rock and roll could meet without either being diminished. Although Lowe recorded as a solo act for contractual reasons, he was really one-fourth of Rockpile, a traditional rock-and-roll band that also featured guitarist Dave Edmunds, a producer and revivalist with a resume even longer than Lowe's; guitarist and singer Billy Bremner; and drummer Terry Williams.

The band Rockpile was widely perceived as a meeting ground for Edmunds's aggressive traditionalism and Lowe's wry wit, and although the group's dedication to "pure pop" contains elements of both styles, their shared vision of straight-ahead rock and roll grounded in the fifties but relevant a generation later outstripped anything either of them has subsequently accomplished separately. Rockpile was a more formidable band live than on record, but their sole LP as a unit, *Seconds of Pleasure,* lived up to the myth. In interviews around the time the record came out, Edmunds claimed that the title was a reference to Lowe's sex life, and what was in the grooves had the same semi-serious attitude as Edmunds's dig.

As usual on Lowe or Edmunds records, most of the original tunes were by Lowe, though this group of compositions was a bit crabbier than usual: Songs about overweight lovers and unrepentant future-ex-husbands stood alongside the usual fare of barbed love and lust songs. Also, this record sounded different from its predecessors, particularly in the close vocal harmonies throughout (early pressings of *Seconds of Pleasure* included a four-cut EP of faithful Everly Brothers numbers for those who didn't get the message), and the requisite Chuck Berry song, "Oh What a Thrill," was for once an *obscure* Chuck Berry tune (though not as obscure as "Dear Dad," from Edmunds's worthy *D.E. 7th*). Throughout *Seconds of Pleasure,* Rockpile push notions of what is traditional, what is acceptable in such limits. For this record at least, they acknowledged none.

Number Seventy-One

Mott the Hoople
Mott
Columbia, 1973

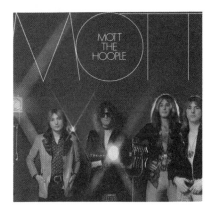

Ian Hunter loved Bob Dylan too much for his own good, but that didn't stop him from eventually coming up with his own worthwhile ideas. His early albums for Atlantic leading Mott the Hoople (the name comes from a Willard Manus novel) were derivative and a bit tuneless, although some of the cover versions (Doug Sahm's "At the Crossroads," even Sonny Bono's "Laugh at Me") suggested some intelligence at work, and anyone who could think up the title "Death May Be Your Santa Claus," let alone a song that justified that title, certainly had great promise.

The group (among the members, guitarist Mick Ralphs, later of Bad Company, provided some crunchy, witty riffs, but Hunter clearly pulled the strings) grew immensely when it moved to Columbia. Its first LP for the label was produced by David Bowie, but for once the then-Ziggy Stardust did not turn out thin hard rock masquerading as thinking man's hard rock. Bowie gave the group one of his best songs ever—"All the Young Dudes"—and introduced them to the Velvet Underground, yielding a definitive version of Lou Reed's romantic "Sweet Jane."

Having upped the ante (and wisely dropped Bowie, whose production effectiveness was always a question mark, especially two LPs in a row), Mott the Hoople promptly cut a great album, *Mott*. The sound was crisp and detailed; the piano on "All the Way from Memphis" jumped between the cracks in the drums of Dale "Buffin" Griffin. Hunter's singing had gained enough emotion for its distance to seem less off-putting (the Pet Shop Boys do the same thing nowadays) and Ralph's guitars were now part of the song, not a barrier to them. "All the Way from Memphis," a tale of spiritual and geographical dislocation that was featured prominently in Martin Scorsese's *Alice Doesn't Live Here Anymore*, set the tone

135

for an album of inspired self-reverential songs ("Hymn for the Dudes," "Ballad of Mott the Hoople," and many more) and also set the stage for future spirited self-chroniclers like the Replacements and the Mekons.

Some of the songs on *Mott* are generalized and chilling ("Violence" and "I Wish I Was Your Mother"), but it's "Ballad of Mott the Hoople," a cockeyed statement of purpose, that means the most today. Over backing that is somewhere between sloppy and nonexistent, Hunter lists all that he feels is wrong with his career, his band (he names his compatriots), and the absurd idea of being a grown-up in a touring rock-and-roll band. He talks about his stupid predicament, but adds that he could never do anything else. Hunter was in a fix, but even in his despair he knew that hopelessness could generate great songs. Still, none of these great songs was a hit, and the band soon fell apart.

Number Seventy-Two

Steve Forbert
Alive on Arrival
Nemperor, 1978

Reconstructed folkie Steve Forbert's debut album is one of the most charmingly self-deprecating yet ambitious folk-rock albums of the late seventies—it's an acoustic punk manifesto. *Alive on Arrival* is, loosely, a concept album, detailing the young Forbert's move from Meridian, Mississippi (Jimmie Rodgers's hometown, for those of you looking for signposts), to New York City, where he hooked up with Ramones manager Danny Fields and earned himself a genuine recording contract; the song titles ("Big City Cat," "Tonight I Feel So Far Away from Home," "You Cannot Win If You Do Not Play") outline the story.

Most of the songs feature a full band, but Forbert's lanky acoustic guitar and gleefully frazzled voice is always front and center. On the cheerful-in-spite-of-itself love song "Goin' Down to Laurel," he deploys syllables like bombs: "They tell me this great life can always . . . end," he sputters, and the pause before that last word leaves us hanging with excitement and unknown travail. "What Kinda Guy?" is a ragged acoustic rockabilly workout with Forbert wrenching out phrases, tossing in a pair of harmonica asides to break up the unrelenting irony.

The fiercest cut of *Alive on Arrival* is the more low-key and frankly fatalistic "It Isn't Gonna Be That Way," a mournful examination of lost possibilities that nevertheless argues for struggle and pluck. The tune has echoes of Van Morrison and in a strange way even Otis Redding, and for a moment rightly places Forbert in their company.

Number Seventy-Three

John Lennon
Plastic Ono Band
Apple, 1970

How bad can you hurt?

Plastic Ono Band hasn't aged well, but it remains one of the most audacious, iconoclastic albums in all rock and roll. The former Beatle was reacting against everything possible here, everything from Paul McCartney to his dead mother, from God to the lush sound of *Abbey Road*, and he sought to strip everything to its core. Lyrics were streamlined, instrumentation was sparse, and Yoko's pretensions were almost totally absent.

Much has been spouted about the lyrics on this album, the anger and desperation that encircled Lennon, and two decades on, *Plastic Ono Band* continues to justify such promotion. The one-word-title songs, "Mother," "Isolation," "Remember," "Love," and especially "God," represent lyrics that are not merely insular, they're self-involved. Arthur Janov's primal scream therapy, the proto-New Age belief system with which Lennon was infatuated at the time, infects the ostensibly confessional words so much that sometimes the listener feels embarrassed, like an inadvertent eavesdropper. Yet let's be honest, that's the way Lennon wanted it, since he was such a natural manipulator of lyrical masks. As his subsequent work with Elephant's Memory would emphasize, the personal, not the political, was his *metier,* which is why the brutal "Working Class Hero" is the greatest of his political songs. It focuses on one man and then jumps out, in the tradition of the song's obvious antecedent, Bob Dylan. (In "God," Lennon sings, "I don't believe in Zimmerman." Ha.)

As with most great rock and roll, more important than what Lennon sings is how he sings. Phil Spector produced this record in association with John and Yoko, but you'd never know it. Lennon's voice is remarkably effect-free, and the only immediately apparent sound augmentations

138

are echo and reverb that add weight and tension. The lack of typical Spector kitchen-sink production methods is telling, and suggests that for once Lennon held sway over their joint productions. Lennon was going back to his roots musically as well as emotionally on this album; as Tim Riley writes in *Tell Me Why*, the echo and reverb on *Plastic Ono Band* are Lennon's way to summon up the sound of his beloved Sun-period Jerry Lee Lewis. Throughout this album, Lennon is as pained as the Killer was when the latter burrowed into the barbed-wire country-and-western standards that ate at his soul. The pastoral-delight cover photo on this album is wishful thinking.

Number Seventy-Four

The Persuasions
Chirpin'
Elektra, 1977

Nowadays, it seems only collectors and nostalgia buffs care about doo-wop. Otherwise, doo-wop only pops up in jeans commercials (or Color Me Badd videos, which are the same thing) or show-off Bobby McFerrin records, and then in watered-down form. If acoustic music can bring musicians and songwriters closer to the essence of their material, a strategy born in rock with *The Basement Tapes,* then a capella music, unencumbered by any ornamentation, can with the right voices bring one to all sorts of cores, emotional and musical.

The Persuasions were veterans, fifteen years into the music, when they recorded *Chirpin',* the greatest doo-wop record ever made. Jimmy Hayes, Jerry Lawson, Herbert Tubo Rhoad, and Joseph Russell sang a capella in one form or another since the early sixties. They had enjoyed the patronage of some big rock stars, who got them record deals and gave them backup-singing gigs. Although they got close to the big time, they never got away from straight doo-wop; rumor has it they turned down a deal with Warner Brothers when label executives insisted they add a full band to their mix. *Chirpin'* is an album overflowing with experience, with commitment, and with a sense of possibility. They take on songs from sources as diverse as Tony Joe White, the Dominoes, Sam Cooke, and Jackie Wilson (as well as the inevitable "Papa Oom Mow Mow") and intertwine them in a larger story as inextricably as their voices coalesce.

The Persuasions recorded *Chirpin'* as a quartet, although some of the weird power on the record comes from the fact that on several tracks the arrangements are for five-voice harmony (the group initially thrived as a quintet), and we listeners fill in the blanks. Nothing needs to be filled in on the record's most outstanding new track, "Looking for an Echo," a

140

tune presented as autobiographical, telling the story of the group's commitment to direct emotional expression in spite of everything, concentrating on their early years. Although they never spell it out, the message of the song and the whole album is These Things Matter to Me No Matter What You Think. The song is a love song to the music, a declaration of fidelity, a remembrance of the thrilling discovery of a street corner symphony, and the knowledge that talent is never enough. "Looking for an Echo" is earnest, but its key line is that such a site was "a place we almost found." The Persuasions use that "almost" not as a reason to give up after fifteen years, but as an impetus to keep on moving.

Number Seventy-Five

Junior Walker and the All-Stars
Compact Command Performances
Motown, 1986

Except for the Contours, Junior Walker and the All-Stars were the only successful Motown band who were consistently able to make noise without frequent intervals of Gordian politeness. Autry DeWalt ("Junior") Walker had no business being at Motown. His touchstones were the saxophone-driven urban rhythm and blues of the early fifties; he would have fit in perfectly with any number of Ike Turner's famed Memphis bands.

But Walker was more than just a throwback. Walker thrived at Motown because he was willing, perhaps even anxious, to mix his party rhythm and blues with the more disciplined approach advocated by Motown dictator Berry Gordy. The friction between these styles and the surprising complementarity between them is what made Junior Walker and the All-Stars a brilliant, forward-looking band, and not just a charming anachronism doomed to a lifetime of southern university frat parties.

"Shotgun," from 1965, was Walker's first big hit and it set the pattern for the group's sound until later in the decade when they began to favor more deliberate tempos. Each instrument—particularly Walker's fluid saxophone and rougher voice, and drummer James Graves's incessant thwack—moved forward with the inexorability of a steamroller, adding up to a massive grunge, an enormous honk, that conformed to Motown style (in James Jamerson tradition, the bass is the lead instrument) yet powered across the speakers more emphatically and less buttoned-up. Other hits, like "Do the Boomerang" and "(I'm a) Roadrunner," extended this method to include both more rhythm and more pop. Walker's records were not cluttered, but they were full of battles. Clarence Clemons is still trying to figure it out. Walker was remarkably adept at slowing down his post-R&B/pre-funk mix to middle tempos—"What

142

Does It Take (To Win Your Love)'' places him in the Motown Zeitgeist without oversmoothing his sax or his vocal, but the raucous uptempo tunes are the ones that still fill oldies-station formats (I could do without the Burton Cummings composition here, though). Walker was a crucial figure in bringing pure, wild rhythm and blues to the fore in an environment that usually necessitated that such tendencies be checked at the door.

Number Seventy-Six

Fela Ransome Kuti and the Africa '70
Roforofo Fight: Music of Fela
Editions Makossa, 1975

A few years ago, when Fela Kuti, the timeless veteran Nigerian political and Afropop iconoclast, was finally allowed back into public after a decade battling his extremely undemocratic government, time had come for a reassessment of some of his less-well-known work. (For his best-known work, neophytes are directed to *Zombie*, a 1977 album reissued by Celluloid.)

In the early seventies, singer, saxophonist, and keyboardist Kuti released two dozen or so albums that were steeped in his elliptical riffs, his relentless call-and-response vocal arrangements, and his superstud/ superpolitician persona. Almost all his records from that period are worthwhile (though ultimately they are a bit interchangeable), and *Roforofo Fight: Music of Fela* is the most representative and lively of them. As with most Kuti records, there are only two songs on the album, the fifteen-minute title tune and the seventeen-minute "Go Slow." But don't be put off—this isn't an Afropop "In-a-Gadda-Da-Vida." Both songs give Kuti and his eleven-piece band (one of his smaller units) adequate time to enter a groove, cascade around its rounded edges, ride it up and down until it is all but exhausted, and leave it stronger and more vibrant for all the attention. (Go for the burn.) Kuti's lyrics (in translation; he hadn't yet started declaiming in pidgin English) are a series of amiable enough chants that advocate inarguable social action, such as refusing to be complacent. That was enough for the Nigerian government to take him down. Two years after this album was released, Nigerian soldiers destroyed his land, broke his hands, raped some of his wives, and helped his mother to an early grave. The pillage led Kuti to even more overt politics and even more forceful musical workouts.

Number Seventy-Seven

Arthur Alexander
The Greatest
Ace, 1989

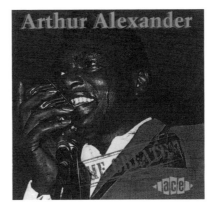

Alabaman soul singer Arthur Alexander is noted mostly as a writer. Of his four charting hits, all are better known in others' versions. The Beatles covered "Anna (Go to Him)" and "Where Have You Been (All My Life)," the Rolling Stones intoned "You Better Move On," and Jerry Lee Lewis danced through "Every Day I Have To Cry." It's no surprise that the Beatles, the Rolling Stones, and Jerry Lee Lewis have better musical taste than nearly all of us, and it's worth going to the source of such standards as "Soldier of Love" and "A Shot of Rhythm and Blues."

The Greatest is a twenty-one-cut compact disc of his most lasting recordings, his early sixties work with Dot. Alexander's father was a blues guitarist, and although Arthur Jr.'s voice and songs were softer, the blues influence made its way into the terse (for the time) arrangements: The strings on "Anna (Go to Him)" never stray toward schmaltz. Alexander's voice was less threatening than traditional blues voices, but it was straightforward and open enough to call up all sorts of emotion without over-revving. Alexander glided through his songs, even the terrifying "Call Me Lonesome," a tale as violent as any in soul.

Alexander was later overtaken as a soul singer and writer by the folks at Stax and Goldwax, but in many ways Alexander set the pattern for his children. His early recordings for Dot (and his session the year earlier for the blues label Judd) were among the first that united backwoods singing with backing, mostly by white accompanists, that leaned more toward country-phrased gospel. On *The Greatest*, almost as decisively as on Ray Charles's and the Drifters's Atlantic compilations already heralded, we hear a school of soul being born. Ironically in this case, the name of the first band supporting Alexander was Dan Penn and the Pallbearers.

145

Number Seventy-Eight

B.B. King
Live at the Regal
ABC, 1964

Belated traditionalists U2 may have just gotten around to canonizing the greatest non-Chicago-identified postwar urban bluesman who isn't John Lee Hooker, but anyone who cares about the unbuttoned passions of the blues or the blues side of rock and roll will respond to the master's work. Born in Indianola, Mississippi, King grew to maturity devouring Charlie Christian and T-Bone Walker records before he became a Memphis disc jockey in the mid-forties, not long before he began putting his knowledge to work in the studio for his own recordings. His very first sessions, cut for the Bullet label while he was still hustling Pepticon on Memphis station WDIA, are a bit subdued and jazzy but he quickly outgrew his accompanists.

Armed with a Gibson hollow-body he named Lucille, King finally reached a broad audience during the blues revival of the sixties. The path was cleared by his many imitators in rock and roll; Michael Bloomfield and Eric Clapton are only two of the leading white players who took cues from Lucille. As a rule, King flourished in front of a live audience, even if he was sometimes a tad too ingratiating. King's easy prowess as a showman and easy-rolling entertainer who can take a crowd through peak after peak stands as a model for all modern performers in all forms of popular music. *Live at the Regal*, a paradigm of pop performance, is brilliant throughout, but the signal moment comes toward the end of a reading of John Lee Hooker's "It's My Own Fault." Scraping for a conclusion, King unearths pain upon pain, and then soothes us all. King's greatest performances didn't flinch from horror, but they also never denied the possibility of salvation. Here, he gives us everything.

Number Seventy-Nine

The Morells
Shake and Push
Borrowed, 1983

Cynics might tag this charming independent-label record as one of the last stands against the final, successful charge of corporate rock. Along with the other thirty-nine people who bought *Shake and Push*, I say feh. The timelessly unpretentious *Shake and Push* is not simply a leftover from a looser age, although that is part of what it represents. It was recorded in Springfield, Missouri, by the unlikeliest of quartets, featuring new-wave veteran (and future cult producer) D. Clinton Thompson sharing vocal chores with Lou Whitney, a bar-band veteran whose back-cover photo suggested that he was twice Thompson's age.

Of course, they have no problem stomping on common ground. The first track, "Gettin' in Shape," is a paean to fitness as Gary U.S. Bonds might have shouted during his first heyday at Legrand. Whitney and Thompson are both spectacularly adept, guileless guitarists who never settle for screamingly clean roots-rock place settings when they can throw darts through rhythm spokes. The two wrote many durable tunes that clamor for interpretations—the most vivid might be the rockabilly "Red's," which honors the greasy cheeseburger joint that adorns the album's cover—but the two most lasting songs here are contributed by Ben Vaughn, the finest songwriter in Camden, New Jersey. His "Growin' a Beard" is a no-nonsense rave-up that praises the delayed arrival of facial hair, and "The Man Who Has Everything" anticipates Bruce Springsteen's "Ain't Got You" with a more fleshed-out skiffle arrangement. The Morells push, kick, and shout, and welcome their own commercial oblivion. They have resurfaced occasionally over the last decade, usually under the name the Skeletons, and *Shake and Push* was recently reissued on CD by the good folks at East Side Digital.

Number Eighty

Sam the Sham and the Pharoahs
*The Best of Sam the Sham and
the Pharoahs*
MGM, 1967

The back cover of this glorious compilation portrays four strangely attired people running around a tree. They don't seem to know why they are doing this, but they are enjoying themselves immensely, and seem committed to continuing the action until they fall down. This image serves as an ideal metaphor for understanding Sam the Sham and the Pharoahs.

Sam the Sham, whose real name is Domingo Samudio, is a Dallas-born crazy (last we heard he was a street preacher in Memphis) who loved raunchy, laconic rock and roll of the most giddily mindless variety, and his sidemen—Ray Stinnet, David Martin, Jerry Patterson, and Butch Gibson—were consistently able to carry him to a demented part of frat-rock heaven. They recorded briefly for something called Dingo Records and then moved to MGM.

Sam the Sham and the Pharoahs are best known for their pair of Number Two smashes, "Wooly Bully," a masterwork of indecipherability that made "Louie Louie" sound like an enunciation class, and "Li'l Red Riding Hood," a hormone-laced fairy tale with a happy ending. If you're guessing an enormous Kingsmen influence on these organ-heavy folks, you're right. Hits aside, the modest gifts of the band were surprisingly malleable, as showcased on charming, wacked-out cuts like "The Hair on My Chinny Chin Chin," "El Toro de Goro (The Peace Loving Bull)," and "(I'm in With) The Out Crowd." All these songs were defiantly insubstantial, and all held out deep meanings to those with the right bent.

Historical note: Every cut on *The Best of Sam the Sham and the Pharoahs* was produced by legendary Sun Records sideman and sometime Elvis Presley composer San Kesler. You go figure the connection.

148

Number Eighty-One

Charlie Rich
*Original Hits and Midnight
Demos* (Charly, 1985)
*Don't Put No Headstone on
My Grave* (Zu Zazz, 1986)

Taken together (and one imagines they will someday soon show up on the same compact disc, thanks to the Colin Escotts and Richard Weizes of the world), these two albums make the best available case for Charlie Rich long before Billy Sherrill dressed up the singer, songwriter, and pianist in flowing—sometimes overflowing—string arrangements. Rich came to Sun late in its heyday, and was groomed to be a millionaire songwriter. He wrote both sides of a single for Sun's biggest star of the time, Jerry Lee Lewis, but the Killer's scandal came between Rich and his Cadillacs.

Rich's first record came out in 1958, after a few false starts, mixed with some turns as a session pianist, including a session for Jerry Lee. (If you can figure out why anyone other than the Killer was requested to play piano on a Jerry Lee record, please contact me via the publisher.) Rich didn't score his first hit, "Lonely Weekends," until 1960.

At Sun, Rich displayed an eclecticism that rivaled the Killer's—and that of Sam Phillips—though more high-toned and high-minded. Rich came from a jazz background but recorded blues, rockabilly, pop, country, and schmaltz with equal fervor. The first album of the double *Original Hits and Midnight Demos* features his best-known and sturdiest Sun sides ("Who Will the Next Fool Be" is the king); the second album offers up nineteen demos and alternate takes that are more randy and less encumbered.

All that mars Rich's released Sun singles is a predilection for intrusive backup choruses, strings, and horn sections, which is exactly what *Don't Put No Headstone on My Grave* aggressively mixes out in the service of pure Rich. The first side of this record presents the complete session that resulted in the inconceivably unreleased title track, Rich's most defiant blues. The flip side pushes forward eight of Rich's best-known Sun performances with the garbage sliced out. Finally hearing what Rich was like behind all that is really an education in what goes on behind closed doors.

Number Eighty-Two

Southside Johnny and the Asbury Jukes
Hearts of Stone
Epic, 1978

Southside Johnny Lyon is the American equivalent of Graham Parker, and not just because of their occasional vocal similarities. Both approach their music as a life-or-death proposition, both got that idea from the amazing commitment to material they heard in sixties rhythm-and-blues records recorded in Memphis and Muscle Shoals, and both were energized by punk although neither were punks. At their cores, Lyon and Parker were soul singers.

After two good-to-great albums (*I Don't Want to Go Home* and *This Time It's for Real*) that presented soul classics alongside new sacrifices to the tradition by old pals Bruce Springsteen and Steve Van Zandt, Southside Johnny and the Asbury Jukes released the greatest soul record to ever come out of New Jersey. Everything on *Hearts of Stone*, particularly the writing (no oldies here, just nine Van Zandt and Springsteen originals) and the production (by Van Zandt)—was more taut and less constrained by what the band had already been able to achieve onstage.

The Asbury Jukes had improved tremendously in terms of discipline and stamina, but they did get help from some ringers: E Street Band drummer Max Weinberg pushes the beat throughout, and anyone who's heard the *Darkness on the Edge of Town* outtake of "Hearts of Stone" is reasonably certain that the version here is that take with Lyon's voice and some extra guitar by Van Zandt grafted atop. And who's the singer responding to Lyon's call on "Trapped Again"?

Whoever played what (as with most albums, you can ignore the list of credits on the back cover), the band swiftly burrows inside these songs, most of them romanticized tales of fractured love, and leads Lyon to their

151

souls. Not that Lyon needs any help. His singing on *Hearts of Stone* is his least chatty and his most believable, and his artless gruffness makes his and Van Zandt's soul dreams come true.

Number Eighty-Three

Dwight Yoakam
Just Lookin' for a Hit
Reprise, 1989

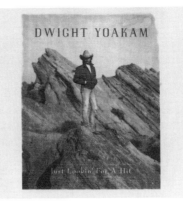

Dwight Yoakam is the greatest young figure in country music today, yet he's far from satisfied. He grew up in Pikesville, Kentucky, made his reputation in southern California, and rightly detests the Nashville machine that made him a star (if you had a brain, would you want to be associated with Billy Sherrill?). Although Yoakam shot to the top playing some country classics—his first hit was a faithful version of Johnny Horton's "Honky Tonk Man"—he has done his best to construct records that alternate hard country with broader ideas. All Yoakam's records are worthy (my favorites are the extremely evil *Buenos Notches From a Lonely Room* and the rugged *If There Was a Way*), but the greatest-hits set *Just Lookin' for a Hit* is the most representative of Yoakam's iconoclastic methods, considerable accomplishments, and limitless future.

Yoakam's records are built around the catch in his nasal twang and the guitar overlays of producer Pete Anderson. Yoakam's natural affinity is to the bare-bones sixties recordings of Merle Haggard and Buck Owens, and it's no accident that Buck himself shows up for a duet on Owens's "Streets of Bakersfield." That track is ideal for Yoakam; its harsh beats and accordion are in direct opposition to Nashville countrypolitan slush, and its outlaw lyrics would make Chet Atkins blush. *Just Lookin' for a Hit* is full of work identified with previous country-identified iconoclasts, performers like Elvis Presley and Gram Parsons, and Yoakam's own compositions are all outside-looking-in outbursts that simultaneously celebrate and condemn his chosen status.

Yoakam is most imposing here thrashing through Dave Alvin's "Long White Cadillac," a tale of a dying Hank Williams, sung from Luke the Drifter's point of view. Clipped guitars distort and entwine, drums

153

explode twice to the bar, and Yoakam hums, screams, and slides through the tale, begging for deliverance, well aware that there will be none. In the coda, Yoakam nearly slices his acoustic guitar in two, shredding all around him. As the song finally crashes closed, Yoakam stifles a laugh and spits out the word "psychedelic." He knows he has a country hit, and he knows that it's really too harsh to be considered country. Such a moment is not country music—its attitude is nothing but rock and roll.

Number Eighty-Four

John Mellencamp
Scarecrow
Riva/Mercury, 1985

As Owen O'Donnell and I pointed out, Johnny Cougar was a joke. On the albums he recorded between 1976 and 1982, he offered pleasant radio music, but nothing worth pondering once the next song began. In 1983, the multiplatinum *Uh-Huh* changed that. "Pink Houses," the album's standout, irrevocably upped the ante; simultaneously an affirmation of traditional U.S. values and a damnation of what they've become, it melded Mellencamp's populist politics with an anthem-like backing. He couldn't maintain that high level for the length of an LP, but such songs as the Bobby Fuller Four hommage "Authority Song" raised expectations.

On *Scarecrow*, Mellencamp accepts the challenge even as he hangs onto a vestige of his previous incarnation (overreach, obviousness, dumbness). At its best, *Scarecrow* brings Mellencamp's sixties-rock fixation and his fiercely patriotic distrust of Power into the muck of the modern world. A sense of responsibility and a need to atone for past missteps pervade *Scarecrow*. On the midtempo "Minutes to Memories," Mellencamp tells the story of a kid stuck on a bus listening to an old man rail. Easing into its final verse, Mellencamp hushes his band and in a voice just above a whisper, he shifts the tale from third to first person, damns himself for patronizing the old man, and passes the old man's words to his own son. (At the other extreme, some of the lyrics buried in Side Two are syntactical hilarities.)

Like many rockers, Mellencamp worships *Exile on Main Street* (no argument here); the musical and production values of the Rolling Stones have had a strong influence on his band. Throughout this record they teeter on the edge of becoming a cover band but stay on the right side of the line.

The sound is low-tech, built around Kenny Aronoff's pseudo-Max Weinberg snare drum. The sinewy mix is all drums and guitar, with bass and keyboards emphasized sparingly and strategically.

On *Scarecrow*, Mellencamp grows up. He sees an American dream dying around him, but he intends to go down fighting—even if authority always wins.

Number Eighty-Five

Bunny Wailer
Hook, Line 'n Sinker
Solomonic, 1982

Jamaican singer Neville Livingston, who took the name Bunny Wailer when he joined with Bob Marley and Peter Tosh (their Wailers were a fledgling vocal trio expanding the boundaries of ska, the precursor of reggae, in the early sixties), spent the late seventies reminding reggae fans in the States of his supple, burnished tenor on an album of Wailers oldies and an exultant memorial LP for Marley. Problem was, as melodic and graceful as *Sings the Wailers* and *Tribute* were, they suggested that Bunny Wailer was reduced to expertly savoring his past.

Not to worry. Wailer's keen understanding of the intertwined sources of soul, hip-hop, and reggae provided a still-unduplicated fusion breakthrough with *Hook, Line 'n Sinker.* His soul-reggae synthesis retains the insouciant slink of reggae but grafts on Famous Flames horn blasts and Steve Cropper guitar accents that punctuate and paraphrase the beat. On "Riding" and "Soul Rocking Party," Wailer rides and parties over Sly and Robbie's hybrid polyrhythms like a smiling Rasta surfer (the latter number even features a rap—not a toast, a rap).

Most witty is a variation on the rhythm-and-blues standard (it's so old that nobody's sure who wrote it) "The Monkey," sung from the creature's point of view, in which the singer is ashamed to think that he and man share lineage. The mixing, matching, and rough juxtaposing of styles and narratives fresh from *Billboard* charts with those that date back to pre-colonial Africa is quietly subversive and occasionally hilarious. The little-noticed album (probably because it was released only in Jamaica) is a stirring use of experience by a wise veteran. It demands wider release.

Number Eighty-Six

Artists United Against Apartheid
Sun City
Manhattan, 1985

Sun City isn't like most all-star "cause" records; its passion pervades both the message and the music. (Be serious now. Did you like "We Are the World" for its music? Did you even notice the music?) Steve Van Zandt and company's righteous anti-apartheid ruminations are deeply felt and on target, and this intensity runs through the music behind them. Intentionally or not, Van Zandt and coproducer/hip-hop genius Arthur Baker (de)constructed a veritable State of Pop Music 1985, diving into the disparate genres of rock and roll, art-rock, jazz, funk, and blues and coming up with something wild, inspired, and genuinely new. Most impressive, they did all this by using hip-hop as the common ground for these forms, heralding heady fusions (Aerosmith and Run-D.M.C., Public Enemy and Anthrax) of years to come.

Van Zandt's lyric writing on the various permutations of the title track (two on the LP, more on various singles) is as concise as only the best post-Dylan political rock. He sets the ugly scene ("people are dying"), delineates some relevant issues ("separation of families"), and insists on a response ("I ain't gonna play Sun City.") The many voices that relate this powerful story are stunning in their variety and chilling in their shared sense of purpose. Between the extremes of Darlene Love's dignified cry and Lou Reed's borderline-offkey gallows deadpan, some of contemporary pop's leading figures make clear that this is no empty charity ball.

Backing up the singing is a beat strong and flexible enough to serve as the basis for most of the album, most effectively on Peter Gabriel's atmospheric rumble "No More Apartheid." This beat works as well in a guitar-rock setting ("Version II") as it does in "Let Me See Your I.D.," a dense rap built around Gil Scott-Heron's alternately offhand and incisive obser-

158

vations (that Dylan influence again). Straying furthest from the original track is Bono's "Silver and Gold," in which the U2 singer adopts country blues with the fervor of a new convert and laments the tragedy in southern Africa with a warmth that overwhelms its lack of finesse. (On the down side, this may be the origin of U2's lunatic search for roots in the Mississippi Delta, the wrongheaded hilarity that gave us the film *Rattle and Hum.*)

The Sun City project, which is still very much alive, is about informing and motivating. That we can dance while we're organizing is but one of this record's triumphs.

Number Eighty-Seven

Womack and Womack
Love Wars
Elektra, 1983

Van Morrison has spent a career reinforcing the counterintuitive notion that just because something fits the format of easy listening it doesn't mean that such a song can't be as fierce and unsettled as the harshest rock and roll. Soul music (and though Morrison's invented genre stretches the form, it is indeed soul music) is built partly on the irony of expressing despair in a beautiful manner, and from William Bell to Terence Trent D'Arby, great singers have turned such ostensible discord into masterpieces.

Cecil Womack and Linda Cooke Womack work in this rich tradition, squeezing out passion from arrangements that in most other hands would feel slick. They've certainly got the background to pull this off. Cecil's brother is the great guitarist and writer Bobby Womack (he wrote "It's All Over Now"), and both Cecil and Bobby sang in the family gospel group. Cecil's previous wife was early Motown siren Mary Wells; Linda's father was Sam Cooke. Genetics don't really mean much in pop music—listened to any Julian Lennon or Pake McEntire records lately?—but environment is everything. The Womacks have always lived in a world in which music is cherished, and their familiarity with and love for what they're doing is consistently engaging.

The couple made several wonderful records during the eighties, and this is the finest of them. *Love Wars* is something of a concept album, nine interwoven ruminations on the difficulty in maintaining (and surviving) long-term romantic relationships. "I don't believe in magic," Linda sings in "Baby I'm Scared of You" (a title Prince would later evoke in *The Black Album*'s far more carnal though less frank "Rock Hard in a Funky Place"), but that doesn't stop this duo from trying to imagine a world in which

160

make-believe makes sense. Cecil offers all sorts of comfort in "Baby I'm Scared of You"; all lead Linda to repeat "I need a little more."

As an image extended for the length of a song (and, to a lesser degree, the entire LP), "Love Wars" is surprisingly resilient, from the "Bring it on home/And drop the guns on the floor" couplet in the title tune (a dark spin on a timeless Sam Cooke lyric) to the terrifying recasting of the Rolling Stones' minor "Angie." They're not kids, they plow through their tales of fractured romance with intelligence and irony, and they don't condescend to us by giving us a happy ending. This last point is the likely reason *Love Wars* wasn't a massive hit.

Ah, forget the words. What makes *Love Wars* a record that thrills listeners to the marrow are the vocals of Cecil and Linda (indeed, the most important instruments here are their voices and James Gadson's liquid drums). Their pre-conscious intimacy recalls the casual vocal array of the Band's *Music From Big Pink* and Otis Redding and Carla Thomas's *King and Queen.* The music may soothe, but the ideas behind the music and the lyrics are as smooth as sandpaper.

Number Eighty-Eight

X
See How We Are
Elektra, 1987

High morale was contagious among left-of-center rock-and-roll fans in 1980. The Clash had scored a bona fide hit single off *London Calling*, John Lydon had stormed back with *Metal Box*, and communities across the U.S. were spawning punk bands that were angry with a purpose—even bands that weren't overtly political spit out venom meant to cure complacency. Along with the Clash, Los Angeles's X helped refine the idea that punk was not an outright assault on rock and roll but a deathbed reprieve for it. On their first two albums, 1980's *Los Angeles* and 1981's *Wild Gift*, singer/songwriter Exene Cervenka, singer/songwriter/bassist John Doe, guitarist Billy Zoom, and drummer D.J. Bonebrake didn't damn tradition so much as wrestle it to a draw. If you accept forebearers like Robert Johnson and Elvis Presley, you have more of a sense of how far you have to go to breach the outer boundaries of the territory.

Zoom scrawled whiplash guitar lines that sounded like Chuck Berry's Airmobile pushing 300 m.p.h. (with nods to Gene Vincent and Johnny Ramone as it whooshed by them), and Bonebrake concentrated on hitting a snare drum as hard and precisely as possible. But it was the songwriting of Cervenka and Doe that set X apart. Some of the sketchy tunes on their debut now sound overly enraptured with urban-sprawl gloom and beautiful-loserdom, but by *Wild Gift* they were able to direct both their vocal and songwriting harmonizing to championing fidelity—to an idea, to a way of life, to a lover. (Cervenka and Doe were married.) They made everyday relationships sound like a tightrope walk, exhilarating if you made it across, but don't bet on it. For three albums after *Wild Gift*, the group was unable to keep on track for an entire LP. Their lack of direction, exacerbated by the separation of Cervenka and Doe, and the departure of Zoom, led fans to ready obituaries.

But X chose the treacherous course of retrenchment, rebuilding the band with a new producer (Alvin Clark) and new guitarists. *See How We Are* was their edgiest, most sustained set. Guitarists Dave Alvin (who left the Blasters to join X and soon skedaddled) and Tony Gilkyson (who strengthened Lone Justice before it turned into a crypto-art band) didn't try to replicate Zoom, and Cervenka and Doe did not need to write around Zoom's style anymore (Zoom's inability to keep up with them when they slowed their tempos a fraction was a frequent stymie). "4th of July," Alvin's lone original, was sharp country-rock, and the sly "Cyrano de Berger's Back" set Bonebrake's echoey drums against dark, country-and-Eastern six-string tones. Alvin and Gilkyson recognized what Zoom added—the pile of guitars on "In the Time It Takes" was a plain echo of Zoom's reverberating lower-register lead lines—but they stayed clear, on the perimeter, determined not to stand in someone else's shoes.

Even more important, after four albums of thanking her voice teacher on lyric sheets, Cervenka finally justified the announcements. Aggravated dissonance had been her pervasive vocal tic, but she developed enough flexibility to sing a deadpan couplet like "I'm stuck to you like flies to glue/Or trash on Broadway" (from "You") and give equal weight to both the romantic and the lurid parts of the simile. X still posited themselves as outsiders, and half a dozen LPs on, it did not sound like an act. *See How We Are* kicked off with "I'm Lost," in which Doe and Cervenka, skidding across Bonebrake's ferocious beat, sang as a homeless pair with dour resistance. "Look left and right and then run like hell," they counseled in the feverish "Left and Right"; "I'm in that other nation," they admitted in the ironic "Holiday Story." They didn't fit in.

A need for community and a simultaneous disaffiliation from any home intertwined most violently in "4th of July" and "See How We Are." In "4th of July," written by Alvin, Doe was trapped in a relationship he couldn't fathom. "She gives me her cheek when I want her lips/But I don't have the strength to go," he sighed, then looked out the window and saw fireworks shooting by him. It was Independence Day, there was a celebration going on, and he wanted them to be part of it. He suggested they venture outside, invoking Bruce Chantel's "Hey! Baby" over and over, hoping that his invitation (and the rousing accompaniment) might prod her. But the house stayed dark, his cigarette withered away, the two of them were too frightened to love, to move toward or away from each other.

"See How We Are" was more glum and more ambitious. It was a letter from many jails, both a standard plea that tried to cement what was left in common with the wife on the outside and an oblique comment on the unavoidable internal prison. The band rose in high guitar/synthesizer crescendos and then eased back into the grumbling-bass lowlands, giving Doe and Cervenka enough room to state their case without leaving them too alone. With every terse line, Cervenka and Doe tried to piece together disparate injustices as fragments of a larger horror. The images collided and resolved into their harmony repetitions of the title line, as much a plea as a demand. Downer though it was, *See How We Are* was suffused with help and a shout: It doesn't have to be this way.

Number Eighty-Nine

The Kinks
Greatest Hits
Rhino, 1989

Their legions have wasted a rain forest's worth of oxygen claiming that the Kinks are either (a) the greatest of all British rock-and-roll bands, or, failing that, (b) equals of the Beatles and the Rolling Stones. Both assertions succumb to the usual hyperbole of cult worship, but the Kinks at their best were a formidable, crude band whose energy trampled over their pretensions.

The Kinks at their best turned out to be the Kinks at the earliest (this fact is denied by the group's most loyal fanatics, which should prove the assertion all by itself). The most taut of their conceptual albums (1968's *Something Else* and the 1971 *Muswell Hillbillies*) showcased Ray Davies and company broadening their musical concerns without getting bogged down in the theatrical trappings and fey affectations that often characterize their work when they're not intent on rocking out. But never did they make their points so boldly, so quickly, or so vividly as they did in their original incarnation. Their cult to the contrary, they didn't enlarge their lyrical lens, though that's no sin; from the start their sights were set on the right targets. The Rhino *Greatest Hits* is a vastly improved version of Reprise's original early-years best-of that came out in 1966, eighteen tracks from 1964 to 1966 that are as brutal as anything generated by the British Invasion.

The great early Kinks records centered on the conflict between Dave Davies's artless guitar sprints (he must have spent *a lot* of time learning different ways to play the Kingsmen's "Louie Louie") and his brother Dave's precise dissections of other people's pretensions. To Ray's credit, he usually took on the failings of those above him in social and economic class in songs like "A Well Respected Man" and its superior sequel "Dedicated Follower of Fashion." Supposed spokesperson for the underclass W. Axl Rose—who hates everyone not as fortunate as he—could learn a great deal from these records. Also to Ray's credit, his interest in economic realism rarely got in the way of spare lyrics in songs like "Who'll Be the Next in Line," "I Need You," and the ferocious "Till the End of the Day" that demanded tight, trenchant words worthy of Dave's power chords. Dave guaranteed himself a spot in the Rock-and-Roll Hall of Fame merely by dreaming up the five sharp chords at the beginning of "You Really Got Me," but in the period chronicled by *Greatest Hits* he developed into a superb accompanist whose direct, straightforward, crunchy style either smoothed or roughened his brother's stories. For someone who seemed to spend half his time onstage trying to bash in his brother's head with his guitar, Dave as a guitarist was remarkably empathetic to Ray's rapidly expanding visions. On "I'm Not Like Everybody Else," a startling demand for independence that makes self-pity sound like a rousing, worthwhile possibility, voice and guitar embark on a dialogue in which little is resolved but everything is definitively dissected.

Alas, this was about as far as they got. Those in search of the pick of the Kinks' work from their later years (and I don't want to make it sound like their ideas completely evaporated after 1966) at Reprise are directed to *The Kinks Kronikles*, a double-album from 1972, which skims the best off their premier conceptual albums: songs like the nostalgic "Victoria," the beautiful and nostalgic "Waterloo Sunset," the angry and not at all nostalgic "David Watts," and what has become their signature tune, the innocent "Lola."

Number Ninety

Mekons
The Mekons Rock 'n' Roll
A&M, 1989

The Sex Pistols trashed as many of rock's traditions as they could, but they also forged a few. The one that lasted longest was ambivalence about stardom. When punk turned into new wave (which then turned into the Knack), it was easy for the original punks to say they wanted to shun the brass ring. But eventually they got tired of playing to the same eight hundred people every time they came to a town. The great ones, like the Clash, found a way to keep the feeling but broaden their base. The rest jettisoned punk as being anything but a fashion move; they turned into business people. The Mekons were the only original punk unit to make it into the form's second decade with their ideals intact and their vision clear. With *The Mekons Rock 'n' Roll*, they tried for a mass audience after years spent torturing themselves with their inability to secure one.

One of the industrial-punk outfits to leap out of Leeds, the Mekons dissolved in the early eighties after the audience for their jagged sounds dwindled to the band itself. After a reunion EP's worth of experimentation, they reemerged reinvogorated with *Fear and Whiskey*, a magnificent, expectation-shattering album that owed more to the trepidation and resignation of honky-tonk weepers and Childe Ballads than to any punk forebearer. They sang of being disenchanted and dislocated—a typical song title was "Hard to Be Human Again"—with uncommon ferocity and specificity. On the slew of fine recordings they did after that (many of them, as well as all of *Fear and Whiskey*, preserved on the CD-only *Original Sin*), they refined their updated attack and developed their own underdog mythology. They knew they were playing for no one by rock-industry standards—sales hovered around ten thousand copies—and they drew strength from their permanent underdog status.

167

The Mekons Rock 'n' Roll was not merely the group's most clearheaded recording. Their belated first major-label album, it was a hand held out to the mainstream rock audience. Yet this rapprochement came with conditions. The record's cover art shook down to depicting a defaced Elvis Presley, which perfectly expressed the Mekons' ambivalence. They loved rock and roll, but they hated the means by which the music was disseminated, so they filled their most mainstream album with unremitting rants against the pop-music industry. The record started with the bracing thrash of "Memphis, Egypt," a terrific, energized tune filled with ideas like "The battles we fought were long and hard/Just not to be consumed by rock and roll." The Mekons' best songs were more obsessed with the group's inexplicable lack of commercial success than even those of the Replacements. On the rollicking country-rock "Club Mekons," led by Susie Honeymoon's fiddle, singer Sally Timms (one of three lead vocalists, along with guitarists Tom Greenhalgh and Jon Langford) equated rock and roll with cheap sex and necrophilia. When Timms sang "I saw a world where the dead are worshipped/The world belongs to them/Now they can keep it," she shied away from that world at the same time she demanded entry.

This desire to have it both ways was made explicit between the cascading riffs and rhythms of the blaring "Blow Your Tuneless Trumpet," a down-home scorcher that suggested the Clash merging with Fairport Convention. For all that they said they hated rock and roll, the Mekons were awfully familiar and comfortable with the form. Even without the challenging rhetoric that suffused all twelve cuts, *The Mekons Rock 'n' Roll* was grand, stirring stuff; the music on "Empire of the Senseless" and "Amnesia" stood tall and anthem-like without the overlay of oratory. "Only Darkness Has the Power" was a romp with the thrust of early-eighties power pop, with more of an edge; "Learning to Live on Your Own" gave Timms a chance to glide through a post-punk flip side to Petula Clark's wide-eyed "Downtown"; and "Someone" spiraled out from its stuttering guitar and drums introduction, sustaining listeners through repeated onslaughts. Indeed, the unencumbered drumming of ex-Rumour stick man Steven Goulding was the Mekons' secret weapon.

The year 1989 was a good one for grizzled rock veterans. From the Rolling Stones and Bob Dylan to Lou Reed and Neil Young, old guys offered records notches above what anyone expected at that late date. By 1989, the Mekons had tumbled into the category of older performers finding new ways to get a hearing while staying true to their innocent punk origins. They succeeded, ready to be heard on the usual rock-biz terms, but by then there was no one left to hear them. By their next album, the fine *Curse of the Mekons*, they were once again recording for an independent label, dancing furiously on the margins of the music industry.

Number Ninety-One

The Blasters
Hard Line
Slash/Warner Brothers, 1985

Granted, most proponents of roots rock became as much of a joke as the dinosaurs they sought to displace or at least reenergize. Many bar bands said they loved the music of Chuck Berry when what they were really trying to do was get a beer company to finance them. For most, roots rock was a fad to exploit and then move on from. The most distressing example of this was Rank and File, an extraordinary country-punk band, second only to Jason and the Scorchers, who eventually deteriorated into a sub-mediocre heavy-metal band.

The Blasters, labelmates of Rank and File, never yielded. None of their five albums (not counting a recent posthumous compilation) made much commercial noise, but never did they make any attempt, overt or otherwise, to dilute their sound, rockabilly-tinged Chicago-style blues, into something the little girls were said to understand. Even more heartening, they got better with each album, so much so that their final LP, *Hard Line*, solidified their status as one of the decade's greatest bands.

The Blasters came from a long rock-and-roll tradition of friction-prone brothers whose mutual ambivalence manifested itself in high-energy, great-sounding messes. Phil Alvin was the singer, as well as a sometime mathematician and devotee of Sun Ra, who would grit his teeth and squeeze his eyelids together as he sang, sweat pouring down his face. His powerful voice, a gruff tenor that picked up ideas while singing along to Sonny Boy Williamson records, seemed oblivious to all around him, except the particular pain it was at that moment describing. Phil's brother Dave was the band's requisite songwriter and guitar-playing Einstein. Dave grew up believing the American myths we'd all like to believe are being protected for us: equal opportunity, all the stuff we hear every four years. Unlike most of us, Dave learned how to articulate his anger over those in power who treat ideals like platitudes for sale.

The political songs on *Hard Line* take on this all-encompassing disappointment—"Dark Night" uses whiplash guitar to shout the tale of a racial murder, and the sarcastic "Common Man" is an all-purpose antipolitician rant. But the real fury against diminished expectations comes in the personal songs. Two collaborations with X's John Doe, "Just Another Sunday" and "Little Honey," swiftly and subtly examine how lives lived in lies can evaporate at whim, and the revived traditional "Samson and Delilah" takes on all sorts of spiritual and romantic abandonment. The album climaxes with the horror story "Rock and Roll Will Stand," the tale of an aging rocker who "almost had a hit," but didn't, mostly because the semi-talented performer sold out at the first opportunity. No matter how speedy the song's pace, no matter how piano and guitar jabbed each other, no matter how much Dave and Phil fought in the mix to get their points across, the song wisely capped a career with no commercial potential. The Blasters weren't stupid. They played "Rock and Roll Will Stand" with outrage and security. Platinum success was never going to happen the way they were going, they knew, and they weren't about to lie to make it happen. R.I.P.

Number Ninety-Two

Ritchie Valens
Ritchie Valens
Del-Fi, 1959

Many rock and roll fans, even thoughtful ones, argue that Ritchie Valens was a minor performer, a one-hit wonder whose legendary status is due only to his bad luck in air travel. It's true that Valens didn't record much before his death at the absurdly young age of seventeen, but what he did cut has lasted, and the one major hit he enjoyed (from the grave, anyway) will surprise most people; it was the elemental, marrow-raw "Donna," not "La Bamba."

Richard Valenzuela is the only major performer in rock-and-roll history whose debut album was released posthumously, which should give you a sense of how short the guy's career was. But he was an astonishing prodigy guitarist, deeply influenced by Eddie Cochran, and he sang straight and harsh like he was auditioning for Art Rupe, Little Richard's shepherd in the studio. It makes sense that a teenager's influences would be immediately apparent on his debut LP. "That's My Little Suzie" reinterprets Larry Williams's "Bony Maronie," which appears five tracks later on *Richie Valens,* and "Ooh My Head" recontextualizes the only slightly superior Little Richard song "Ooh! My Soul." Valens's most famous composition, "La Bamba," a reluctant rocking up of his Chicano heritage that has inspired hundreds of cover versions and one hilariously bad film, is the basis of the Beatles' arrangement of the Isley Brothers' "Twist and Shout," and for nothing other than keeping Los Lobos in business, the song deserves our lasting appreciation. For defining a field of rock-and-roll exploration that would inspire such tremendous Latino-rock performers as Chan Romero, The Perimers, Cannibal and the Headhunters, and The Midniters, "La Bamba" deserves to be recognized as a landmark.

172

Some cuts range farther afield. "In a Turkish Town" marries the romantic and the borderline xenophobic (my wife adds, "I like the way the guitar goes *twang*"), which is weird considering "Donna" was written in part to defend himself from a girlfriend's racist father. "Dooby Dooby Wah" is a nonsense song just as profound as "Be Bop a Lula," plus it's faster.

Number Ninety-Three

Lone Justice
Lone Justice
Geffen, 1985

Midway through T Bone Burnett's set opening for Richard Thompson at New York's Bottom Line sometime in the winter of 1984, he brought a shy-looking young woman onstage. "Eighteen and never been, uh, kissed," he announced. Maria McKee looked intimidated, but she went on to sing with such conviction and force that Burnett, a first-rate performer himself, was wise enough not to try and share the center microphone with her. Applause, she left, the set continued, I filed her name.

In the months that followed, the buzz about Lone Justice, the band McKee founded with guitarist Ryan Hedgecock, built to enormous proportions. They're the best band in L.A., we heard, and East Coast boosterism intact, we snickered at how little that must mean. They're mixing country and rock, we heard, and we feared Poco. And then they appeared with a debut album that surpassed the hype.

Lone Justice's country-rock tag makes sense if you consider Creedence Clearwater Revival's "Up Around the Bend" or Bruce Springsteen's "Darlington County," songs that acknowledge their roots and then rock out like landslides, country-rock. A genuine country sensibility does run through the ten songs on *Lone Justice*—after all, this is a band that started off doing George Jones and Rose Maddox covers—but they love too many kinds of music to settle for country-rock alone. "Sweet Sweet Baby (I'm Falling)," written by McKee with Heartbreaker keyboardist Benmont Tench and former E Streeter Steve Van Zandt, is pure white-soul pop, and the album's first single, a take on Tom Petty's "Ways to Be Wicked," is an exemplar of mainstream rock that finds emotional cores. "I can watch how your eyes light up while you're walking me through hell," McKee sings, and the brazen/wry resignation in the lyrics is countered by the Steve Cropper-influenced rhythmic lead lines of Heartbreaker guitarist Mike Campbell. The originals, by McKee and bassist Marvin Etzioni, are equally direct. Her "Wait 'Til We Get Home" and his "You Are the Light" are flip sides of the same story, hard church-rock in the spirit of Aretha Franklin backed with soft, brooding country gospel, asserting scolding of a misbehaving lover backed with an equally desperate plea for strength from the same person. Both sound like a part of the same real life.

On all these song, producer Jimmy Iovine seems to push everything to the front of the mix. McKee's big voice, inspired by Chrissie Hynde yet recalling "Jolene"-era Dolly Parton, Don Heffington's restrained and powerful drums, and many other elements all battle for lead space, while Hedgecock's multiple guitar overdubs carom all over without things ever getting cluttered. Seldom has so much joyous noise been presented so clearly.

Strangely, this apotheosis of mainstream rock and roll was a dud—both of its singles petered out in the pop chart in the seventies—and the group went through many permutations, finally turning into what sounded like a Stevie Nicks tribute band before McKee called it quits. She currently records as a solo artist, slowly gliding back toward her original triumph.

Number Ninety-Four

Ennio Morricone
*The Original Soundtrack to
"Once Upon a Time in the West"*
RCA, 1972

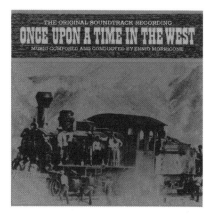

Out of silence, a lone, distorted electric guitar begins its cry. The air around its wriggling notes swelters. Barroom shutters flutter in the dry wind, a stagecoach zooms out of town so as to escape the imminent confrontation. When the dust clears, two worn men, twenty feet apart, stand frozen. They stare at each other, legs spread, right hands hovering near hips. A harmonica bounces off the guitar, and the tension rises. The street is desolate. First one and then the other reaches for his six-shooter. The guitar screeches. One man falls to the ground, dead.

We've seen this sequence or something like it in hundreds of Westerns ranging from the taut *High Noon* to Elvis's misbegotten *Charro.* They all climax with the gunfight that the audience has been screaming for. In the best of them, these blasts—with or without the help of an electric guitar—release both the actors and the folks in the theater. Starting in the late sixties, Sergio Leone, an Italian, directed a series of smart, barbed Westerns that took on the form's conventions only to tweak them obliquely. The most lasting of these films, *The Good, the Bad, and the Ugly* and *Once Upon a Time in the West,* suggest epic reinventions of American West mythology that make their protagonists all the more human by depicting them as vividly and starkly as cartoons.

Leone had many collaborators in these "spaghetti" Westerns, but the director's most important associate was the conductor and composer Ennio Morricone, who came up with overpowering scores that became strong supporting characters themselves. You remembered how the films sounded as much as how they looked. For example, during the extended opening credits of *Once Upon a Time in the West,* three fierce-looking gunmen await the arrival of hero Charles Bronson's train so they can kill him. Leone has them take up different positions in the train station; one passes the time by hunting down a pesky fly, another dodges a leak in the station roof. Here, the rhythms of Morricone's music are meant to approximate the clip-clops of steady hoofbeats. To add to the tension, he cuts off the song in mid-note several times. Each time, you (and the characters) are primed for action. By the last time, everyone is ready to burst. For Morricone, who has scored some three hundred films and television shows, the music comments on the action and even initiates it.

Of all the hundred albums in this book, *The Original Soundtrack to "Once Upon a Time in the West"* is probably the one that its creator is least likely to identify as rock and roll. Morricone's work occasionally resorts to literalness or sentimentality (as it has recently in his scores for *The Mission* and *Casualties of War*), but when Morricone understands the film before him and is committed to emphasizing appropriate elements of it without editorializing, he can turn bad films into good films, good films into great films, and great films into masterpieces.

Morricone pulls this last trick in his score for *Once Upon a Time in the West*. Recorded in 1969 but not released until 1972, it's the high-water mark of Morricone's long collaboration with fellow Italian, director Sergio Leone. The film, nearly three hours long, is Leone's most skillful and comic; Morricone's score is his most terse and brutal. The film is the boldest and broadest of all spaghetti Westerns and one of the few to understand how deeply environment determines character. It is a revenge tale (Charles Bronson searches for Henry Fonda, the outlaw who killed his brother), with all sorts of cosmic and comic interludes adding gravity and relief. Morricone's austere, troubled score is integral to the film; Leone edited and cut the film to this majestic music, rather than the traditional other way around.

Morricone uses an orchestra throughout *Once Upon a Time in the West*, but it is the crucial addition of repeated motifs on electric guitar (and, to a lesser degree, harmonica) that makes this record conform to a wide definition of rock and roll—and unlike even most good soundtracks you don't need to see the film to enjoy the record. The overamplified electric guitar—Morricone has clearly been exposed to *Are You Experienced?*—slices through the orchestra and provides a jagged counterpoint to the quiet, deliberate settings, both audio and visual. A lonely guitar slashes through like Hendrix on the prairie. The thirteen tracks on this soundtrack, some of them full-bodied excursions, some quick mood pieces, clearly and unequivocally evoke the sound and the spirit of the romanticized Old West. The pain and pleasure, the tension and release on this record make this closer to rock and roll than most of what's in the Top Ten whenever you read this.

Morricone continues to work with Leone—their most recent project is *Once Upon a Time in America*—and with the possible exception of the budding symbiosis between David Lynch and Angelo Badalamenti, theirs is the most fruitful of all director-composer combinations today.

Number Ninety-Five

The Who
Meaty, Beaty, Big, and Bouncy
Decca, 1971

Until Keith Moon died, shaking everyone but his surviving bandmates back to their senses, most fans of the Who considered Moon and his collaborators, Pete Townshend, Roger Daltrey, and John Entwhistle, ongoing geniuses. Indeed, the Who gave us some fine music in the seventies. *Who's Next* is a titanic and still-unequaled expansion of what the marriage of rock and technology might yield, *Quadrophenia* is half-great, and subsequent individual tracks, like "Who Are You," suggested that rumors about their being washed up might be premature. But facts are facts: The group reached their apex by 1971, and the downhill slide (which, alas, did not end upon Moon's senseless demise) was inexorable and depressing. Throughout the seventies and eighties, Townshend and company sought to curry critical favor by reaching into their archives and showing how deep their catalog was. The only problem was that nearly all the material from the vaults worth bringing out was recorded before 1971.

The Who in the seventies were indecisive and inconsistent; through the eighties and into the nineties they are a joke. But in their first seven years, they could rise to heights just shy of the Beatles and the Rolling Stones. *Meaty, Beaty, Big, and Bouncy* is a definitive survey of this period.

Except for *Who's Next* and maybe *Live at Leeds* and *Tommy*, none of the Who's albums were stirring from beginning to end. The Who were primarily a live band, and on record they were (discussing them in past tense may be wishful thinking) primarily a singles band. *Meaty, Beaty, Big, and Bouncy* collects nearly every great non-*Tommy* track the Who recorded prior to *Who's Next*. "A Quick One While He's Away," a nine-minute proto-*Tommy*, is the only exception. This isn't a greatest-hits set, at least for U.S. fans—only one of these fourteen numbers, "I Can See for

Miles," was a Top Ten hit—yet it is a superb display of how this band that started out playing loud, adequate versions of soul hits quickly developed into a louder, groundbreaking unit. This is not a cross-section of major tracks; this is damn near everything from the period that matters.

Meaty, Beaty, Big, and Bouncy starts with the scratchy guitar chords of "I Can't Explain" and bounces around with Moon's unpredictable drums that break every existing rule about tempo and meter yet always show up on time. Moon dances around the song and band, taunting both, daring them to follow him, always resolving his own messes. The feedback pyrotechnics of Townshend and Entwhistle and the macho histrionics of Daltrey are simply their brave attempts to be heard above Moon. (Everyone, including the man himself, calls Townshend a genius, but Moon led this band, which goes a long way toward explaining why the group turned rudderless as he was more and more unable to contribute, finally abandoning them.)

They all did get heard, and perhaps a quarter of a century later what is most impressive about these songs are the taboo or absurd subjects they tackle: "Pictures of Lily" is explicitly about masturbation; "The Seeker" and "Substitute" are about debunking myths, rock and otherwise; "A Legal Matter" tells of a creep who impregnates his girlfriend and swiftly skedaddles; "I'm a Boy" tells of a child forced by his mother to cross-dress; and Entwhistle's only song here is about trying to kill a spider. These issues were hardly addressed at all in pop before the Who, and never in such detail or wise humor. On *Meaty, Beaty, Big, and Bouncy*, a young, brash band creates a new world.

180

Number Ninety-Six

The English Beat
Special Beat Service
I.R.S., 1982

One of the most heartening changes punk wrought—and one of the few that didn't evaporate almost immediately upon contact with the mainstream—was the advent and sustainment of the 2 Tone label, the greatest Do-It-Yourself label in nearly two decades. (Although none of the aggressive dance bands on 2 Tone played a mix that was anything resembling punk, their genre-busting ideas would have been inconceivable without punk to suggest that it was possible.) 2 Tone was an independent record label out of Britain that showcased the marvelous ska revival of the late seventies and early eighties. As the original punks exhibited a dramatic affinity for reggae, the next line of punks felt close to ska, the slippery uptempo dance music from Jamaica that gave birth to reggae.

The best-known of these bands was the Specials, whose greatest work (particularly "Free Nelson Mandela") did not come until years after 2 Tone's impact, like punk's, had dissipated. But the one group from this movement whose impact still grows (even a stodgy man stuck in his own past like Pete Townshend performs their songs) was the Beat, known on these shores as the English Beat.

The English Beat were about more than ska. They epitomized the 2 Tone ideal of black and white kids, men and women, united by love of music and mutual respect, all dancing. Their stage demeanor was that of a tight dance band—singer Dave Wakeling and toaster Ranking Roger ran crowd control, bassist David Steele and guitarist Andy Cox slid across the left side of the stage at high speed trying not to bump into each other, and so on. This ensemble playing was impressive live and even more so on their records, particularly their third set, *Special Beat Service*. Their debut album *I Just Can't Stop It* pushed the limits of ska beats to include songs about male bonding and begging Margaret Thatcher to quit as well as songs associated with Smokey Robinson, Prince Buster, and Andy Williams; the follow-up, *Wha'ppen?*, was more of a downer, though on songs like "I Am Your Flag" they were able to fill dance floors and minds simultaneously.

Special Beat Service far exceeds either of its predecessors. There are songs that owe their souls to reggae, like "Pato and Roger a-Go Talk," as well as many other weighty tunes that convey a deep understanding of not only ska, but also juju, *mbaqanga,* and all sorts of Caribbean pop forms. Lyrically, the canvas is also wider. After two albums stocked with overtly political songs, *Special Beat Service* is full of snaking songs about the impact of public policy on personal behavior. Rather than go on about politics—on *Wha'ppen,* the English Beat had taken that tack as far as it could go without appearing petulant—here they travel from Parliament to the bedroom and the living room, and cuts like "I Confess" and "Save It for Later" brilliantly dissect lives so sapped of energy by the outside world that they have nothing but anger to bring home. The outlook is bleak, and more powerful for it.

Having peaked, the English Beat did the appropriate punk thing and broke up. Ranking Roger and Dave Wakeling enjoyed some success, both together and separately, while Steele and Cox, whose contributions to the band had been consistently underestimated, went on to found the Fine Young Cannibals, whose *The Raw and the Cooked* took Prince-derived pop further than anyone other than the Purple One himself.

Number Ninety-Seven

Paul Kelly
Post
Mushroom (Australia), 1985

Nobody knows who Paul Kelly is—and he's great! Granted, the Australian songwriter and singer is something of a derivative performer, or at least his influences keep popping up like pimples. Kelly sometimes seems like a rock-critic-invented mixture of Joe Strummer, Elvis Costello, Bob Dylan, Graham Parker, Bruce Springsteen, and a half-dozen other significant white male rockers, but this is not why he is so little known in the U.S. Three of his records have come out stateside (*Post* is one of four others that have not), and their eclectic arrangements (Kelly seems to be a big fan of *Sandinista!*) and pretensions to literature (Kelly named one album after a Raymond Carver short story) have seemed forbidding to many.

Yet there is nothing dense about Kelly, a Woody Guthrie fan who aspires to similar plainspokenness. His gestures and observations are tiny and reserved. The American rock audience yearns for exaggerated motions—sax players who can spin their back on a stage floor are in great demand nowadays—and Kelly's talents are too honest for that.

Post is Kelly's third album. He normally records with a band, now called the Messengers though its members previously answered to the Dots and the Coloured Girls, but *Post* is a solo acoustic album that emphasizes the dark side of life. Before you start yelling *Nebraska,* know that the pessimism here is more specific than the broad-minded Springsteen would ever allow. (Also know that Kelly gives himself the marvelous luxury of occasional accompaniment, however spare.) Many of the songs here are lyrically grounded in the first stages of recovery from drug addiction. "White Train" and "Blues for Skip" are explicitly about heroin, and all sorts of junk—drugs and otherwise—thwart the soft vocalist throughout the record.

The soft singing is never intended as quiet comfort. The singer in "Adelaide" reimagines his childhood, all detail and foreboding ("Dad's hands used to shake but I never knew he was dying/I was thirteen, I never dreamed he could fall"), and when he stumbles into the present as if it is a bad dream, he tosses off lines like "I own this town" to convince himself that someone is listening to him. In "Incident on South Dowling," a junkie helplessly watches his lover overdose before him, and quickly ponders the layout of the tiny apartment they shared. Little events, tragic results.

The meanest song on *Post* is its truest. A self-satisfied rock-god-in-training sings "Look So Fine, Feel So Low," the tale of an up-and-comer living off the kindness of an innocent young woman ("She buys me things/She wants to take care of me/And all I gotta do is sing, sing, sing") while a millimeter under the surface he detests her ("She's so easy to impress/ When she asks me dumb questions/All I gotta do is say 'yes, yes, yes'") for his predicament. Kelly's character sings in a voice so drenched in derision he is oblivious to his inhumanity. The title lines are attempts to show remorse, but the kid is kidding. What the kid doesn't know is that by revealing himself he has ensured his eventual eviction. He looks so wise, but he's really a fool. These deceptively complex characters are the folks Kelly wants to write about, and their multidimensional nature is part of why their stories don't ring on radios from coast to coast. Kelly subsequently rerecorded rousing full-band versions of many of the songs on *Post*, and those takes are often exhilarating. They're great performances. But on *Post*, they're revelations.

Number Ninety-Eight

Tina Turner
Private Dancer
Capitol, 1984

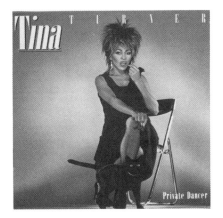

Snuck into the middle of the depressing eighties, 1984 was an amazing year for pop music; the two most popular albums of the year were also the two best: *Purple Rain* and *Born in the U.S.A.* But Prince and Springsteen didn't have the year to themselves, even if they made Top Forty radio painless for the first time since Lyndon Johnson was president. (And it's been a dead zone since then.) Except for Elvis's resurrection from Hollywood, so mammoth that it is beyond categorization, *Private Dancer* represents the greatest comeback in American pop music.

As the vocal half of Ike and Tina Turner, the former Anna Mae Bullock was a force of nature, an unrelenting singer whose greatest hits—Phil Spector's kitsch-en-sink masterpiece "River Deep Mountain High," a two-hundred-miles-per-hour romp through John Fogerty's "Proud Mary"—were confrontational rapprochements disguised as love songs. The duo stopped having hits, their relationship deteriorated into well-documented ugliness, and by the early eighties Tina was reduced to performing at corporate conventions.

Tina's fans were a rugged bunch, suffering through duets with a sleep-walking Chuck Berry and an incorrigibly washed-up Rod Stewart, and many of these fans were fellow performers. The Rolling Stones gave her some work, but her return originated in a strange corner. Martyn Ware and Greg Walsh, British synthesizer boys who made their name in the Human League and Heaven 17, talked her into the studio to record Al Green's "Let's Stay Together." Ware and Walsh's shared reputation was as disco purveyors with a light touch and wry wit (how else could they have come up with a dance hit called "Fascist Groove Thing"?), and the lush post-disco settings they erected around her eased her into all sorts of radio formats without succumbing to corporate conventions.

So what? Arrangements don't matter; little on *Private Dancer* matters save the singing of the woman on the cover. A particularly strong song inspires her to greater heights: Ann Peebles's "I Can't Stand the Rain," John Lennon's "Help," and best of all "When I Was Young," a knowing outtake from these sessions saved for a B-side that made the Animals' original sound silly.

Turner sings like a woman in the second half of her life, all wisdom and experience, no time for reflection or regret. She sings with the ferocity of someone making up for a decade's lost time, and even the work of song-writing hacks like Mike Chapman, Holly Knight, and Mark Knopfler can't stand in her way. Her performance of boring compositions like "Better Be Good to Me" and "What's Love Got To Do With It" are outstanding, shining exemplars of how in rock and roll, commitment, and guts can crush anything in their way. Journalists at the time concentrated on Tina's Betty Rubble hair and her revelations about her past, but they missed the point. When she sang "I might have been queen," she knew she was being extremely ironic.

Number Ninety-Nine

The Kingsmen
The Best of the Kingsmen
Rhino, 1991

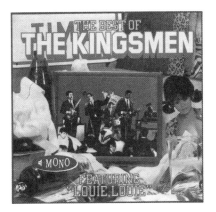

Noise is an essential ingredient in most great rock and roll, as is a healthy dose of incomprehensibility. Hence the status of the Kingsmen's "Louie Louie" as one of the most-loved and most-misunderstood numbers in rock history. The genius of the Kingsmen was to elevate noise and incomprehensibility to humor, a point that they should have made obvious, although everyone from Lou Reed circa *Metal Machine Music* to Captain Beefheart circa any-of-his-albums seems to have missed it.

The Kingsmen are often cited (slighted?) as the definitive trash-rock band. Charting two weeks before John Kennedy's assassination, "Louie Louie" peaked at Number Two, kept from the top spot for six weeks by the Singing Nun's "Dominique" and Bobby Vinton's "There! I've Said It Again," a pair of snoozers that will show up in the second volume of *The Worst* if Owen and I ever get off our asses and write it. Almost as big a hit as "Louie Louie" was "The Jolly Green Giant," a frank celebration of vegetable lust, that made it to Number Four (thus scoring far higher than the Olympics' "Big Boy Pete," where its melody first appeared). But their influence far outstrips most bands who bump into two major hits and a handful of minor ones.

The place to discover and celebrate the Kingsmen is this 1991 compilation by the usually reliable folks at Rhino. The meat of *The Best of the Kingsmen* is the best of the three LPs that came out on Wand in 1964 and 1965, but the few later recordings that complete this set don't pad it.

However, the later songs aren't where to start. Any case for the Kingsmen's greatness is based on four songs—"Louie Louie," "Money," "Little Latin Lupe Lu," and "The Jolly Green Giant." All but "The Jolly Green Giant" are cover versions (and even that lyrical idea began in the mind of some anonymous frozen-food-company PR wizard), but they were all the product of one barbed vision—especially incredible in light of the band's history. The singer on "Louie Louie" was guitarist Jack Ely, who quit the band when he learned that drummer Lynn Easton (under his mother's instructions) had registered a trademark in the name of the Kingsmen. Easton announced to the rest of the band that he was now the lead singer, and he soon had to recruit himself a new backing group. Nonetheless, the new Kingsmen remained committed to junk-rock. Easton sang Barrett Strong's "Money" with enough abandon to put him within shouting distance (and I do mean *shouting*) of John Lennon, and his version of Bill Medley's "Little Latin Lupe Lu" out-raucoused the Righteous Brothers' marvelous original and also provided the frame for the Clash two decades later when they wrote and recorded "Should I Stay or Should I Go."

And then there's "Louie Louie." In 1963, it seemed like every significant Northwest band was playing a version of the then-obscure (it hit no national chart) Latin-tinged original by Richard Berry, a derivative (or precursor, depending on whose calendar you follow) of Chuck Berry's "Havana Moon" that made a long-distance relationship sound like the greatest of all adventures. The Wailers (not the Bob Marley group) scored a local hit with it, as did Paul Revere and the Raiders, who went on to marginally better things. But the Kingsmen's liquid assay, with Ely singing and Easton behind his drum kit, was sonically more impressive because everything in the performance—not just the lyrics—seemed meaningfully garbled. (Not that this matters as anything more than an amusing sidebar, but there was also an insane controversy about the lyrics of "Louie Louie." We all have our own personal version. The lead instruments on the record, and the most unpredictable, are Easton's drums. They slide in and out of lines (as does the vocal, which shows up too early for the third verse and makes the mistake sound intentional, like Paul Reubens falling off his bike in *Pee-Wee's Big Adventure*) and stumble through fills like determined dancers.

The most important words in the song, delivered right before the guitar break, are by far the most direct: "Okay, let's give it to 'em—right now!" That's a sentiment that nobody needs to decode or translate. Michael Stipe notwithstanding, meaningful incomprehensibility is a lot more than just garbled lyrics.

Number One Hundred

The Georgia Satellites
In the Land of Salvation and Sin
Elektra, 1989

The Georgia Satellites garnered themselves a rabid fan base with their first hilarious hit, "Keep Your Hands to Yourself," but even those who had been devotees of the Atlanta-formed group from their inception were shocked by their third album. On *In the Land of Salvation and Sin* the quartet remade themselves into far more than what they already were: the ultimate bar band.

Even after the Satellites emerged as the purest sons of Chuck Berry since the Beatles, their records were cut from the same cloth. As far back as their 1985 EP *Keep the Faith*, they hadn't strayed far from the ideas that first united them. The originals, most of them by singer and guitarist Dan Baird, were feisty and spare, and their bold choice of cover versions acknowledged the likes of Jerry Lee Lewis, Rod Stewart, and the Beatles by playing their songs as fast and as hard as possible (*you* figure out a way to recast "Every Picture Tells a Story"). This was effective and often envigorating, but Baird was a smart enough writer to know that he could only stir the same stew for so long.

Although *In the Land of Salvation and Sin* offered enough agreeable thrashing to satisfy the faithful—the clincher was guitarist Rick Richard's speeding "Slaughterhouse," a long-time staple of their live shows—that was only the beginning. The album's fourteen cuts provided ample opportunity for the band to touch all the old bases and wander toward a few new ones. The Satellites learned how to channel the energy of their engaging barroom rock into a wider variety of forms. Even their tributes—unavoidable from a writer as history-conscious as Baird—gained depth. "Shake That Thing," a Little Feat homage, burnt rubber with its dry, openhearted funk; "Another Chance," a breakthrough acoustic number that overtly recalled *Every Picture Tells a Story*-era Rod Stewart, cruised on the interplay between acoustic and slide guitars and hearty, vulnerable vocals. The improved voices of all members put across such tunes with grace and ease. And *In the Land of Salvation and Sin* showcased the new ways they had developed to work together as singers. On tracks like "Days Gone By" and "Crazy," wild harmonies swooped from above the lead singer and carried the song home. Rolling Stones veteran Ian McLagan added piano on several tunes, and he integrated himself into the band much better than he had on their previous LP, *Open All Night*.

Baird's songs (he wrote or cowrote all but two) capitalized on these performance gains. Numbers as varied as "Sweet Blue Midnight" and "Dan Takes Five," the record's softest and hardest tunes, testified to his expanded ambition. "Sweet Blue Midnight," a tough country ballad with an unexpectedly supportive vocal assist from Nicolette Larson, got to the heart of romantic resignation without turning softheaded. Even if some of their tempos were slower, the Satellites still had no room for sentimentality. At the other extreme, album-closer "Dan Takes Five" was a sweltering rocker that might have seemed of a piece with the group's trademark Berry-derived stomps but was as much a victory of imagination as "Another Chance." Baird conveyed a standard I'm-outta-here-babe tale with an overlay of terror about his newfound independence. In that way "Dan Takes Five" descended directly from Sun rockabillies like Carl Perkins and Warren Smith, who bragged about their brazen exploits only to regret their fight from domesticity.

Most of its tunes (even "Dan Takes Five") had shiny surfaces, and yet Baird's writing on *In the Land of Salvation and Sin* was his darkest and most emotionally complex. The songs were never overdeliberated, propelled by drummer Mauro Magellan, a graduate of the D.J. Bonebrake school of smashing his snare into 4/4 bits. There was intelligence at work, but never at the expense of rocking out. The raucous, good-ol'-boy Satellites still burnt stages to the ground, but their fury was now more stunning because of the fierce ambition that now powered it. From the start, the Georgia Satellites demanded entry into the room that housed the top rank of rockers. On *In the Land of Salvation and Sin*, they knocked down the door.

The Ten Best Rock-and-Roll Books

GREIL MARCUS, *MYSTERY TRAIN*
Now as then, a rigorous, ambitious, inspirational exploration of how the greatest American pop music connects with society, as well as the most clearheaded and comprehensive look at the live Elvis's place in our world, Peter Guralnick's upcoming study notwithstanding.

RODDY DOYLE, *THE COMMITMENTS*
A compact, overflowing novel about the reach of soul music, set in working-class Dublin. Avoid the film, which was made by the director of *Fame*.

MARK SHIPPER, *PAPERBACK WRITER*
An alternate history of the Beatles that some of the group's most hardheaded fans will probably prefer to the real thing.

LESTER BANGS, *PSYCHOTIC REACTIONS AND CARBURETOR DUNG*
Most of the best of an astounding critic who everyone with an attitude tries to rip off.

PETER GURALNICK, *SWEET SOUL MUSIC*
Our finest roots-music observer examines Stax and its ramifications with unparalleled love and reason.

STANLEY BOOTH, *DANCE WITH THE DEVIL*
A tale of the Rolling Stones Countdown-to-Altamont 1969 tour that stunningly reveals the then-Greatest Rock-and-Roll Band in the World and the culture around it.

ROBERT CHRISTGAU, *CHRISTGAU'S CONSUMER GUIDE* (Two Volumes)
Nobody says so much in so little space.

JOHN MORTHLAND, *THE BEST OF COUNTRY MUSIC*
For rock fans, this is the essential introduction to the world of Hank, Lefty, and the Singing Brakeman. Published in 1984, this demands an update.

DAVE MARSH, *TRAPPED: MICHAEL JACKSON AND THE CROSSOVER DREAM*
Marsh's most audacious book and his most wide-ranging, chapters alternating between first-rate dissections of all elements of Michael's myth and open letters to the Gloved One that reveal as much about the sender as the recipient.

PENNIE SMITH, *THE CLASH BEFORE AND AFTER*
A photo book, with hilarious captions by the group members that summons up the spirit of punk better than any other book.

The 25 Greatest Pre-rock Recordings for Rock Ears (in alphabetical order)

LOUIS ARMSTRONG, *JAZZ MASTERPIECES* (COLUMBIA)

These six volumes owe more to the blues than nascent jazz, but misnomer and occasional dumb remix idea aside, here's Satchmo at his early best, with the Hot Five, the Hot Seven, and Earl "Fatha" Hines.

SAM COOKE AND THE SOUL STIRRERS, *IN THE BEGINNING* (ACE, UK)

"Touch the Hem of His Garment" and twenty-two other reasons why Cooke's greatest vocals were recorded before he turned to secular music.

REV. GARY DAVIS AND PINK ANDERSON, *GOSPEL BLUES AND STREET SONGS* (FANTASY)

The two sides of the blues, a street-level equivalent of pairing *What's Goin' On* with *Let's Get It On*.

WOODY GUTHRIE, *LIBRARY OF CONGRESS RECORDINGS* (ROUNDER)

Even the stories that aren't true are real.

HOWLIN' WOLF, *MEMPHIS DAYS* (BEAR FAMILY, GERMANY)

These two volumes document the most austere blues ever recorded, by the genius Sam Phillips. If you want more, *Change My Ways* (MCA) is an excellent collection of Wolf's best after he moved north and the recent *The Chess Box* (MCA) is damn near definitive.

JOHN LEE HOOKER, *BOOGIE AWHILE* (KRAZY KAT, UK)

Stomp.

SAM "LIGHTNING" HOPKINS, *THE GOLD STAR SESSIONS* (ARHOOLIE)

The latter-day country-bluesman's first recordings, and his wiliest, on two CDs.

ROBERT JOHNSON, *KING OF THE DELTA BLUES SINGERS* (COLUMBIA)

I know *The Complete Recordings* is the one to have, but the sequencing on this indomitable masterpiece makes far more sense. Don't buy *The Complete Recordings* unless your CD player is programmable.

LOUIS JORDAN, *THE BEST OF LOUIS JORDAN* (MCA)

The funniest band of all time, and the missing link between Chuck Berry and the blues.

LEADBELLY, *LEADBELLY'S LAST SESSIONS* (FOLKWAYS)

Why the Civil War didn't resolve anything, spread over four albums.

THE LOUVIN BROTHERS, *TRAGIC SONGS OF LIFE* (ROUNDER)

Some call it landmark traditional bluegrass; I call it the scariest album ever recorded.

MOON MULLICAN, *SEVEN NIGHTS TO ROCK* (WESTERN)

Jerry Lee had to learn his best tricks from someone.

CHARLEY PATTON, *FOUNDER OF THE DELTA BLUES* (YAZOO)

Doomy, angry, unmoved; the sound of unrequited everything.

JIMMIE RODGERS, *THE JIMMIE RODGERS LIBRARY* (ROUNDER)

These eight CDs show how much country owes the blues,

and how much country owes the Singing Brakeman. For more, check out *The Bristol Sessions* (Country Music Foundation) and witness the first country music that got past the back porch.

BESSIE SMITH, *THE JOHN HAMMOND COLLECTION* (COLUMBIA)

At the intersection of jazz and the blues, Smith defines several hundred schools of singing. These breathtaking double albums have since been rendered redundant by the label's *Complete Recordings* series.

ERNEST TUBB, *HONKY TONK CLASSICS* (ROUNDER)

Hard-edge country, from a land where friendliness is a double-edged sword.

VARIOUS PERFORMERS, *COUNTRY NEGRO JAM SESSION* (ARHOOLIE)
VARIOUS PERFORMERS, *FATHERS AND SONS: HISTORIC GOSPEL QUARTETS* (SPIRIT FEEL)

These two belong together, because even though they do so in different ways, more than any other records they showcase man's ability to conquer his world.

VARIOUS PERFORMERS, *MURDERERS HOME* (SEQUEL, UK)
VARIOUS PERFORMERS, *BLUES IN THE MISSISSIPPI NIGHT* (RYKODISC)

These two amazing records define the South before the civil rights era: The first covers jailed bluesmen, the second takes in the hopes and fears of brave men just a few steps ahead of the dogs.

VARIOUS PERFORMERS, *THE SUN BLUES BOX* (CHARLY, UK)

Elvis did not create the world; this is the world that created Elvis.

MUDDY WATERS, *DOWN ON STOVALL'S PLANTATION* (TESTAMENT)

Muddy went on to invent Chicago blues when he moved north (*The Chess Box* on MCA is a necessity), but these recordings, made before he left the Delta, are country blues worthy of Robert Johnson or Charley Patton.

HANK WILLIAMS, *THE ORIGINAL SINGLES COLLECTION . . . PLUS* (POLYDOR)

The greatest country singer ever, all his singles. Any questions?

SONNY BOY WILLIAMSON, *DOWN AND OUT BLUES* (CHESS)

Hopeless blues from a man who made Chuck Willis seem like an optimist.

BOB WILLS, *THE BOB WILLS ANTHOLOGY* (COLUMBIA)

Why country used to be called country and western.

The 25 Greatest Box Sets
(in alphabetical order)

James Brown, *Star Time* (Polydor)
Ray Charles, *The Birth of Soul* (Atlantic)
Patsy Cline, *The Patsy Cline Collection* (MCA)
Antoine "Fats" Domino, *They Call Me the Fat Man* (EMI)
Bob Dylan, *Ten of Swords* (Tarantula, bootleg)
Buddy Holly, *The Complete Buddy Holly* (MCA)
Jerry Lee Lewis, *Classic* (Bear Family, Germany)
Little Richard, *The Specialty Sessions* (Specialty)
Carl Perkins, *The Classic Carl Perkins* (Bear Family, Germany)
Otis Redding, *The Otis Redding Story* (Atlantic)
Bessie Smith, *The Complete Recordings* (Columbia/Legacy)
Bruce Springsteen, *All These Years* (Templar, bootleg)
Ernest Tubb, *Let's Say Goodbye Like We Said Hello* (Bear Family, Germany)
Various Performers, *Atlantic Rhythm and Blues* (Atlantic)
Various Performers, *The Complete Stax-Volt Singles* (Atlantic)
Various Performers, *Phil Spector, Back to Mono (1958–1969)* (Abkco)
Various Performers, *The Red Bird Box* (Charly, UK)
Various Performers, *The Sun Blues Box* (Charly, UK)
Various Performers, *The Sun Country Years* (Bear Family, Germany)
T-Bone Walker, *The Complete T-Bone Walker 1941–1954* (Mosaic)
Muddy Waters, *The Chess Box* (MCA)
Hank Williams, *The Original Singles Collection . . . Plus* (Polydor)
Chuck Willis, *My Story* (Demand)
Howlin' Wolf, *The Chess Box* (MCA)
O.V. Wright, *The Complete Recorded Works* (P-Vine, Japan)

The Ten Greatest Bootleg CDs

1. Elvis Presley, *The Complete Burbank Sessions* (Audifon)
Full sessions from the comeback special, on three CDs.

2. Prince, *The Black Album* (various)
Pure funk, available in many configurations, some with extra tracks.

3. Bob Dylan and the Band, *Royal Albert Hall 1966* (Swingin' Pig)
The nastiest live show on earth.

4. Jerry Lee Lewis, *The Killer's Private Stash* (Electrovert)
The Ferriday Fireball's earliest recordings (two years before Sun) and his performance as Iago in a rock-and-roll *Othello*.

5. Bruce Springsteen, *The Saint, the Incident, and the Main Point Shuffle* (Great Dane)
A brilliant February 1975 show in Pennsylvania, on two 75-minute CDs.

6. The Beatles, *Back-Track, Volume 1* (Back-Track)
Will Capitol ever put this stuff out?

7. The Rolling Stones, *Philadelphia Special* (Swingin' Pig)
Touring behind *Exile on Main Street*—what else do you need to know–on two CDs.

8. Prince, *Small Club, 2nd Show That Night* (X)
An afterhours gig on the *Sign o' the Times* tour, a rhythm-and-blues revue worthy of the Famous Flames, on 2 CDs.

9. Van Morrison, *Into the Mystic* (Scorpio)
A classic early seventies show, featuring ''Que Sera Sera''
and ''Hound Dog,'' on two CDs.

10. Jimi Hendrix, *On the Killing Floor* (Swingin' Pig)
Was he great every night? Stockholm 1969, on two CDs.

Ten Crucial Reggae Records for Rock Fans

1. Various Performers, *The Harder They Come* (Mango)
This is the soundtrack to the film that awakened many U.S. and U.K. rock fans to reggae, and features Jimmy Cliff, Toots and the Maytals, and many others.

2. Lee Perry, *Open the Gate* (Trojan)
The deepest of dub, from the greatest reggae producer of all time.

3. Bob Marley and the Wailers, *Catch a Fire* (Island)
See Album Number Forty-Six.

4. Culture, *Two Sevens Clash* (Shanachie)
Apocalyptic, righteous, believable even to non-Rastas.

5. Toots and the Maytals, *Funky Kingston* (Mango)
Lead singer Toots Hibbert went on to record soul music in Memphis; this record is why he fit in.

6. Niney Niney and Friends, *Blood and Fire* (Trojan)
The legendary producer's greatest foggy-headed productions.

7. Bunny Wailer, *Hook, Line, and Sinker* (Solomonic)
See Album Number Eighty-Five.

8. Clement Dodd, *Musical Fever* (Trojan)

9. Clancy Eccles and Friends, *Fatty Fatty* (Trojan)
Two heady installments in Trojan's Producer series.

10. The Cables, *What Kind of World* (Heartbeat)
A vocal group as important to reggae as the Persuasions are to doo-wop.

The Dozen Best Bear Family Releases

Tiny Bear Family Records, in Vollersode, Germany, has established itself as the world's leading reissue label. It puts out massive boxed sets all the time, and has often shamed the major labels with the quality and quantity of its releases. Here's where to start.

Single CDs:
Jerry Lee Lewis, *Live at the Star-Club*
Howlin' Wolf, *Memphis Days*
James Talley, *Got No Bread, No Milk, No Money, But We Sure Got a Lot of Love/Tryin' Like the Devil*
Billy Riley, *The Classic Sun Recordings*
Sonny Burgess, *The Classic Sun Recordings*

CD box sets:
Jerry Lee Lewis, *Classic* (8 CDs)
Ernest Tubb, *Let's Say Goodbye Like We Said Hello* (5 CDs)
Carl Perkins, *The Classic Carl Perkins* (5 CDs)
Bill Monroe, *Bluegrass: 1950–1969* (8 CDs)
Webb Pierce, *The Wondering Boy, 1951–1958* (4 CDs)
Hank Snow, *The Thesaurus Transcriptions* (4 CDs)
Vinyl only:
Jerry Lee Lewis, *The Killer: 1963–1978* (33 LPs, most of them great, believe it or not)

Ten Great Forgotten Singles

Claudine Clark, "Party Lights," Chancellor (1962)
The ultimate one-hit wonder, Clark's shining moment made being left out of a party sound like fun; the inspiration for John Eddie's amazing unreleased "Judy's Party."

Billy Lee Riley, "Flyin' Saucers Rock 'n' Roll," Sun (1956)
The most ludicrously lovely of all rockabilly screams.

Grandmaster Flash and the Furious Five, "The Adventures of Grandmaster Flash on the Wheels of Steel," Sugarhill (1981)
See Album Number Twenty-Five.

Lou Christie, "Lightnin' Strikes," MGM (1965)
Indecipherable, either about love or rape, full of tension and passion. Also not about Sam Hopkins.

Joy Division, "Love Will Tear Us Apart," Factory, UK (1980)
Every dance song out of England in the last decade is anticipated in this number's double-snare rhythms.

The Left Banke, "Walk Away Renee," Smash (1966)
The only great art-rock single.

Television Personalities, "A Sense of Belonging," Rough Trade, UK (1983)
Why Margaret Thatcher was a negative influence on her country.

Sister Wynona Carr, "Life Is a Ball Game," Specialty (1955)
A brilliant gospel-soul extended metaphor in which different saints and temptations play various baseball positions.

Gene Simmons, "Haunted House," Hi (1964)
Mashes "The Monster Mash."

Gino Washington, "Gino Is a Coward," Ric Tic (1963)
One of the most adult songs ever written about committing
to a romantic relationship, and certainly the funniest.

The Best Rock-and-Roll Movies

The Best Films About Rock and Roll
Don't Look Back, featuring Bob Dylan, dir. D.A. Pennebaker
This Is Spinal Tap, featuring Spinal Tap, dir. Rob Reiner
King Creole, featuring Elvis Presley, dir. Michael Curtiz
A Hard Day's Night, featuring the Beatles, dir. Richard Lester
Sign o' the Times, featuring and directed by Prince
Sid and Nancy, featuring Gary Oldman as Sid Vicious and
    Chloe Webb as Nancy Spungen, dir. Alex Cox
The Buddy Holly Story, featuring Gary Busey as Buddy
    Holly, dir. Steve Rash
The Last Waltz, featuring the Band and Muddy Waters, dir.
    Martin Scorsese
The Kids Are Alright, featuring the Who, dir. Jeff Stein
American Hot Wax, featuring Tim McIntire as Alan Freed,
    dir. Floyd Mutrux
The Harder They Come, featuring Jimmy Cliff, dir. Perry
    Henzel
Stop Making Sense, featuring the Talking Heads, dir. Jona-
    than Demme

The Best Films with a Rock-and-Roll Soundtrack
Once Upon a Time in the West, score by Ennio Morricone,
    dir. Sergio Leone
Mean Streets, various performers, dir. Martin Scorsese
Blue Velvet, various performers, dir. David Lynch
Goodfellas, various performers, dir. Martin Scorsese
Performance, various performers, dir. Nicholas Roeg
The Long Riders, score by Ry Cooder, dir. Walter Hill
Batman, score by Prince, dir. Tim Burton

The Twenty Best Rock-and-Roll Singles

1. Jerry Lee Lewis, ''Whole Lotta Shakin' Going On''
2. Marvin Gaye and Tammi Terrell, ''If I Could Build My Whole World Around You''
3. Rod Stewart, ''Maggie May''
4. The Clash, ''Complete Control''
5. Elvis Presley, ''Suspicious Minds''
6. Prince, ''When Doves Cry''
7. James Carr, ''The Dark End of the Street''
8. The Jackson 5, ''I Want You Back''
9. Chuck Berry, ''The Promised Land''
10. Bob Dylan, ''Like a Rolling Stone''
11. The Rolling Stones, ''Jumpin' Jack Flash''
12. James Brown, ''Papa's Got a Brand New Bag''
13. Creedence Clearwater Revival, ''Proud Mary''
14. Aretha Franklin, ''Chain of Fools''
15. Ray Charles, ''What'd I Say''
16. Sly and the Family Stone, ''Everyday People''
17. Arthur Conley, ''Sweet Soul Music''
18. Parliament, ''(I Wanna) Testify''
19. The Righteous Brothers, ''Little Latin Lupe Lu''
20. Bruce Springsteen, ''Tunnel of Love''

ABOUT THE AUTHOR

Jimmy Guterman is the author of four other books: *12 Days on the Road* (with Noel Monk), *Sinéad, The Worst Rock and Roll Records of All Time* (with Owen O'Donnell), and, most recently, *Rockin' My Life Away: Listening to Jerry Lee Lewis*. He has written for a wide variety of publications, among them *Rolling Stone, Spy,* the *Journal of Country Music,* and *PC Week.* He has also compiled and annotated reissue records for many record companies, among them an upcoming Merle Haggard boxed set. His current projects include a study of dissent in the U.S. and a novel about the pop-music industry.